THE ADJUNCT UNDERCLASS

THE ADJUNCT UNDERCLASS

How America's Colleges
Betrayed Their Faculty,
Their Students, and Their Mission

HERB CHILDRESS

The University of Chicago Press
Chicago and London

The University of Chicago Press, Chicago 60637
The University of Chicago Press, Ltd., London
© 2019 by The University of Chicago
All rights reserved. No part of this book may be used or reproduced
in any manner whatsoever without written permission, except in
the case of brief quotations in critical articles and reviews. For more
information, contact the University of Chicago Press, 1427 E. 60th St.,
Chicago, IL 60637.
Published 2019
Printed in the United States of America

28 27 26 25 24 23 22 21 20 19   1 2 3 4 5

ISBN-13: 978-0-226-49666-5 (cloth)
ISBN-13: 978-0-226-49683-2 (e-book)
DOI: https://doi.org/10.7208/chicago/9780226496832.001.0001

Library of Congress Cataloging-in-Publication Data
Names: Childress, Herb, 1958– author.
Title: The adjunct underclass : how America's colleges betrayed their
faculty, their students, and their mission / Herb Childress.
Description: Chicago ; London : The University of Chicago Press,
2019. | Includes bibliographical references and index.
Identifiers: LCCN 2018054735| ISBN 9780226496665 (cloth : alk.
paper) | ISBN 9780226496832 (e-book)
Subjects: LCSH: College teachers, Part-time—United States. |
Universities and colleges—United States—Faculty. | Education,
Higher—United States.
Classification: LCC LB2844.1.P3 C55 2019 | DDC 378.1/2—dc23
LC record available at https://lccn.loc.gov/2018054735

♾ This paper meets the requirements of ANSI/NISO z39.48–1992
(Permanence of Paper).

CONTENTS

NOTE ON INTERVIEW CONFIDENTIALITY

This book employs quotes from interviews I conducted with contingent faculty, postdoctoral researchers, graduate students, and college administrators. These quotes conclude with pseudonymous identifiers such as "Paul, ten-year adjunct" or "Maura, liberal-arts college dean." These are designed to protect the identities of persons whose working lives would be made more difficult if their identities, type of school, or region were known. The pseudonyms are "accurate" only by the presumed gender of their first names, and not by the initials or presumed ethnicity.

THIS IS HOW YOU KILL
A PROFESSION

How did we discard the idea of college faculty? That is, how did we decide to systematically eliminate an entire class of professionals whom we once entrusted to conduct the final distillation of our children into capable, confident adults? How did we come to decide that college teachers didn't deserve job security, didn't deserve health insurance, didn't deserve to make more than convenience store clerks?

It wasn't hard, really.

We discarded college faculty in the same way that we discarded medical general practitioners: through providing insane rewards to specialists and leaving most care in the hands of paraprofessionals.

We discarded college faculty in the same way that we discarded cab drivers: by leveling the profession and allowing anyone to participate, as long as they had a minimum credential and didn't need much money.

We discarded college faculty in the same way that we discarded magazine and newspaper writers: by relabeling the work "content" and its workers "content providers."

We discarded college faculty in the same way that we discarded local auto mechanics: by making all of the systems and regulations so sophisticated that they now require an army of technicians and specialized equipment.

We discarded college faculty in the same way that we discarded bookkeepers: by finally letting women do it after decades of declaring that impossible, and then immediately reducing the status of the work once it became evident that women could, in fact, do it well.

Our contemporary religion of innovation has as one of its tenets the following belief: *Rather than defeat your competition, make your competitors irrelevant.* This is exactly what we see in higher education. College faculty were not defeated after great struggle, after a battle with a winner and a loser. College has simply become redefined, over and over, in ways that make faculty irrelevant. College teaching, as a profession, is being eliminated one small, undetected, definitional drop at a time.

1

WHAT THE BROCHURES
DON'T TELL YOU

It's easy to picture colleges and universities as bastions of stability, as resolute lighthouses of knowledge standing in the face of stormy seas. We think of the ivy-covered walls, the tweed-jacketed professor in his indeterminate fifties and sixties looking out his office window overlooking Old Quad as the freshmen toss a Frisbee around. His tenure protections make things stable, as does the physical investment in that real estate, an immovable campus in place for decades or centuries, the oldest buildings on the oldest landscape in town. Ohio State and Michigan have had their football rivalry forever, as have Cal and Stanford, Army and Navy, Texas and Oklahoma. The mascots and the color schemes and the classroom seats and the faculty lines are eternal, even as generations of inhabitants pass through them, individually anonymous as they enact their assigned role in the enterprise.

If colleges were as constant as we imagine, we'd start to see what we might call a mature ecosystem, named species fulfilling predictable roles. We'd have students in their dorms, and dorm mothers supervising curfew. We'd have faculty in the faculty senate, speaking in genteel Robert's Rules opposition to the deans and provost and president, the executive and legislative branches of government in a genial, perpetual balance of power. We'd have a handful of invisible supporters—bookkeepers and groundskeepers and cooks, all working behind the scenes to smooth the operation. We'd have witty sophomores making sophomoric jokes in the campus paper, and the dean of students and head of campus police shaking their heads in wry appreciation of the ingenuity of pranks, of beer kegs snuck through the gates. The founder's statue would be found, the morning after homecoming, in the president's parking spot, painted in the opposing team's colors.

A quick visit to any college will feel like a historical reenactment, the past lovingly restored and maintained for daily use. But once we go beneath the surface, we discover an ecosystem and mix of species entirely unlike what we might have expected. We find some faculty who don't teach, and some baseball coaches who do. We find a tuition that varies almost from student to student, after financial aid and merit awards and adjustments for part-time status and tuition differentials for popular majors. We find offices that blend functions that used to belong separately to student services and academic services: tutoring centers, undergraduate research programs, study-abroad programs, women's centers, international student centers, and LGBTQ+ centers. We find a bewildering array of quasi-independent research centers, institutes, and public/private partnerships. We find that an extraordinary number of students have transferred into the school or will transfer out, putting pressure on the admissions office to navigate transcripts, and equal pressure on the faculty to make their curricula more or less like everybody else's. We find a ubiquity and constant upgrade of technology.

And, if we ask around, we'll find a significant cohort of teachers and researchers who don't really work there.

I taught as an adjunct from 2009 to 2013. At [community college], I taught first-year seminar and English comp, for $3,200 for a 3-credit course. Those courses had ten to fifteen students each. At [private, not very selective college], World Literature and Writing 1, for about $2,000. Those courses were capped at twenty-three. I tried to teach six courses per semester across both schools at once, plus a couple more in the summer.

Helen sat across from me in the empty lounge at a writers' conference, where she'd responded to my posting to talk about adjunct life. We talked for twenty minutes, and she seemed to get smaller and smaller as she sunk back into the chair, reliving those years in her recent past.

> It was just a huge amount of reading. I was married, didn't have my child yet, and my husband was a medical resident, so he was never around. I was driving an hour or more to get to each school. I was new to the area, I didn't know people, and my husband wasn't around. So I taught, did admissions reading for [elite research university], tutoring, freelancing for a tiny little newspaper. . . . I was just cobbling a lot together. And the money was a meaningful part of our family income, so I really had to do it.

Let's think about what all of this entails. Helen was teaching writing-intensive courses to more than a hundred students each semester, with at least four distinct course types each week, which means she was reading and marking up a hundred essays a week across four different topical areas. There's no way to do that much work in less than sixty hours a week, likely more. With pre-semester course preparation and post-semester grading, the fifteen-week semester becomes an unacknowledged and only partly compensated twenty.

Helen lived fifty miles from one school in one state, and sixty miles from the other school in another state, in an apartment at the middle, near the university hospital where her husband worked. She was on each campus three times a week for each course, and the school wasn't scheduling around her convenience, so she was easily driving five or six hundred miles a week, ten thousand miles a semester.

Even with her graduate degree in English, she had little input into the courses she taught, all designed by others to meet larger curricular goals that she never knew.

With all that teaching, grading, and driving, there wouldn't have been enough time to hold office hours on either campus, though the absence of an office made that possibility moot anyway. So all of the between-class contact with students, the casual coaching that shifts confusion into possibility, took place through e-mail. Each of what could have been brief conversations became a series of carefully crafted writing projects of their own, adding more time to the week.

For all that, she made about thirty grand a year, with no contribution to health care or retirement, no provision of computer or software. It was a stipend that required her to find even more pickup jobs, reading admissions essays, working in a tutoring center, and writing news features.

This is not a recipe for the attentive, patient mentoring of young minds. These are not working conditions that allow for either student or instructor to explore promising side roads, to make false starts that later pay off in surprising ways. This is simply the provision of a product at lowest cost.

Every year, the nearly five thousand colleges around the country send out glossy brochures to anxious high school juniors and seniors in an effort to lure some fraction of them to their institution. They feature photographs of their most beautiful undergraduates on the most beautiful corner of the quad, photographs of those same beautiful students standing one-on-one beside their most attractive faculty in a laboratory. The best features of the institution's surrounding landscape—mountains or forests or urban hipster coffee shops—are prominent. If there's snow in any photo, someone is skiing on it, not slipping across it in a parka with an armload of books.

These documents are obviously sales tools, like the dealer's brochure for the Toyota Camry or the Ford F-150. And just as those brochures never show the less appealing aspects of car ownership—cars idling in big-city commutes, or drivers idling in line at the DMV—there are things about the college experience that are never included in the recruitment material. For example, the highly selective research university . . . the one for stellar students, the one with the world-class faculty . . . won't tell you that your daughter's early courses in academic writing, mathematics, and world languages will almost certainly be taught by someone other than a permanent faculty member.

The brochures from the innumerable lesser-tier schools, the ones that promise upward mobility and access to careers, won't tell you that the majority of your son's faculty will be temp workers. They won't tell you that six, or eight, or even all ten of his first-year courses will be taught by adjunct instructors. They also won't talk much about the related facts that your son will be only 75 percent likely to begin his second year, maybe 50 percent or less likely to graduate. Maybe, at the schools most reliant on temp faculty, a lot less likely.

Any college is a significant business enterprise, with photogenic buildings and grounds, high-performance computing systems, extensive athletic programs, helpful staff in accounting and food service and financial aid, even the advertising team that produces the lovely brochures: expenses that are permanent and unchanging, and easy to market to eager families. The paradox is that the most basic, fundamental feature of college—young people learning from serious thinkers—is the least stable business element, subject to last-minute ad hoc decisions.

There are innumerable terms in use for the vast army of temp labor within higher ed—*adjunct faculty, part-time lecturer, visiting scholar, postdoctoral fellow, professor of the practice, artist in residence.* They all mask the unified underlying condition: working course-by-course or year-by-year, with no guarantee of permanence, often for embarrassingly small stipends, and often for no benefits. The polite language makes the facts harder to see, so let's state it simply: College teaching has become primarily a pickup job, like driving for Uber or running chores for TaskRabbit.

THE QUIET TRAGEDIES OF TEACHING

Just as there are a million part-time college faculty in America, there are a million stories of contingent life. All you have to do is run a Google search using "adjunct," "postdoc," or "contingent" as the first term, and "working conditions," "crisis," or "abuse" as the second term.

Maybe you've read some of those stories. "There is no excuse for how universities treat adjuncts," says *The Atlantic*.[1] "The disposable academic," says *The Economist*.[2] The Center for Labor Research and Education at the University of California, Berkeley, has found that 25 percent of all part-time college faculty are enrolled in some form of public assistance.[3]

But let's get specific.

In fall 2013, the *Pittsburgh Post-Gazette* reported the death of Margaret Mary Vojtko, who died at the age of eighty-three from cancer she could not afford to treat. She died at her home, for which she could not afford electricity. She had taught French at Duquesne University for twenty-five years, never making more than twenty thousand dollars a year for her six or more courses, and never receiving health benefits or retirement contributions.[4]

In fall 2017 the *San Francisco Chronicle* reported that Ellen Tara James-Penney, a professor of English at San Jose State University, slept in her car while teaching her four courses per semester.[5]

> After class, James-Penney said she often drives to a parking lot to grade papers. When it's dark, she'll use a headlamp from Home Depot so she can continue her work. At night, she'll re-park in a residential neighborhood and sleep in her 2004 Volvo. She keeps the car neat to avoid suspicion.

A month later, the *Guardian* upped the ante, with a story of a "middle-aged" adjunct who's turned to sex work to augment her insufficient piecework income.[6]

She first opted for her side gig during a particularly rough patch, several years ago, when her course load was suddenly cut in half and her income plunged, putting her on the brink of eviction. "In my mind I was like, I've had one-night stands, how bad can it be?" she said. "And it wasn't that bad."

The stories are all around us, maybe parked at the end of your street. Throughout this book I'll add to them, for all the good it does.

Here, for instance, is the story of Niccole, who was raised in France, achieving both an MBA in finance and a doctorate in art history from prestigious schools. At twenty-four, she was on the fast track to intellectual success—major curatorial publications on two continents in two languages within the first year after her dissertation. I heard her joy in the work within moments of starting our conversation.

This is a life investigation, it's my way of being. I've always worked hard. I love to teach, to have the conversations. I really like being in the classroom.

But she came to the United States with her American husband so that he could go to graduate school in New York City, and the wheels came off.

I was hired by a friend as a full-timer in design at [a private college] in New York. Other teachers there were from Harvard, Columbia. But the school went bankrupt. So I started at [another private design college in a different state, a four-hour train ride away] part time in 2006, also at [local community college] part time, summer classes at [major research university]. Also, I had a job training horses and teaching riding. So I had a full-time and two-part time jobs.

Along with that, I've been curating art shows, and teaching private seminars through my museum contacts. I was teaching part-time for [another research university] in their continuing education program, doing art history seminars for wealthy collectors. They said to me, "This is crazy, we're paying them a fortune and they're paying you nothing." So now I give private seminars at people's homes, and I get paid five times as much as I did by the university.

[An internationally renowned museum's] director of membership heard a lecture that I gave; she liked it a lot, and so now I do lectures for them occasionally when a curator isn't available. And I got a call to pick up a class two weeks before the semester started at [lower-tier state school]. I taught one course in the fall, two now in the spring, and will have two or three next fall.

This is what faculty life looks like now. In the car, on the bus, on the train, always wondering whether the next semester will be fertile or dry. Living in hope about the promises that are made to keep everyone quiet.

At [the distant design school], I commuted there for ten years. I maxed out as a part-timer, taught the maximum number of credits. I told them I wanted a full-time position, and they told me there was no money to create that; so I quit in summer 2016, after ten years. Then they got the money to create the tenure-track position, and I've applied. [At the current low-ranked state school], there may be a tenure-track line ahead. . . .

Niccole is still positioning herself for a permanent faculty job, though she knows her sell-by date has long expired and her elite dissertation research is fifteen years in the past. But even though that hope endures, she's increasingly clear-eyed about her future, and what she sees as the future of the institutions for which she works.

Getting part-time jobs is easy, but real jobs all go to people with political links within the departments. There's a real catch-22 for publishing when you're an adjunct. You have to travel to do your research, to go to archives; you have to travel for conferences; but instead you take summer jobs. There's no time and no money to publish. I'm already middle-aged; I need to start functioning in a different world.

I don't believe that universities will ultimately need tenured faculty. I had students who asked me about going on to PhD programs, and I always dissuaded them from doing it. My generation is being sacrificed, being crucified for the decisions made by others. There's no value placed on the PhD, and I always discouraged my students from doing it. If you need it for your own intellectual life, and you're independently wealthy, then fine, go for it. But otherwise, forget about it, right away.

The part of tuition that goes to professors is ridiculous. Students may pay a total tuition of $6,000 per class, and you get $100. What else are you in university for, but to take classes from professors? The majority of the tuition should go to that. With a PhD, whatever ways to express yourself get no money. You publish, you get 10 percent of that. You teach, you get a tiny percentage of that. The work is an accumulation of undervalue of your production. And this is the compact we've agreed to, that's commonly accepted. We spend ten years doing research, and we get a fraction of what people make for half of the preparation.

Maybe it's good that the system is coming to a crash.

STORY PROBLEM: WHEN DOES EIGHTY EQUAL NINE?

Here's another story. A friend of mine, Jane, took a job teaching one master's-level course at a school in New York City while also teaching in Boston, reading student papers on the Bolt bus four hours each way, staying overnight on her mom's couch in New York (at age sixty, she was really beyond the age when an accomplished scholar with a PhD should be sleeping on Mom's couch). The New York school had a unionized faculty, and the union had negotiated pay for adjuncts as well, with levels based on credit hours of teaching experience. So when Jane got the contract, her years of teaching translated to a pay rate of a little over eighty dollars an hour. That sounds pretty terrific, but it wasn't. Let's explore how eighty dollars an hour works out to be less than minimum wage.

The stipend was calculated at eighty dollars per *contact* hour. A three-credit course (a fifteen-week class that meets three hours per week) is forty-five classroom contact hours, which means that Jane's stipend for teaching that course was about $3,600. The standard expectation for a three-credit course is that students invest three hours a week in class and six hours outside class—on reading and homework and term papers and such. Every teacher I've ever known has worked *far* more hours than any one student. Between writing the next session's notes and rereading sections of the next book and reviewing and coaching on draft papers and writing emails of encouragement or praise or threat of failure, I've personally never had fewer than five hours outside class per one in it. But let's be conservative, and say that Jane could have gotten away with three hours outside class for every one in student contact. (It was actually far more.) At that rate, her 45 contact hours per semester amounted to 180 actual hours of labor.

All of the course preparation—creation of the brand-new syllabus, selection of readings, coordination with the department chair over learning goals, coordination with the IT department over getting materials onto the course management system—was outside the fifteen-week window. It was work provided for free. Let's be conservative there as well, and call it another eighty hours of course development. Then there's the end of the semester—the grading of final papers or final exams, the agonizing over assigning final grades, the collection and archiving of student work for the college's records. Another eighty hours for that, also outside the window: more free work. Plus the generic email blizzard from the college itself, more or less non-stop, from the department chair and human resources and the registrar.

So the figure of 45 contact hours is a fiction that conceals 350 hours of work, maybe 400, and maybe more. A $3,600 pretax stipend, with no benefits like health care or retirement contributions, spread over 400 hours of work, comes to $9 per hour. In Vermont, where I live, that's just shy of the minimum wage.

Now, of course, if Jane taught that course a second time, and if she were a sloppy teacher who didn't care about her work, then she'd already have the syllabus in the bag and just change the dates. She'd already have the reading list, regardless of which readings were helpful last semester and which ones weren't. She'd have jettisoned almost all of the serious homework for quizzes, to reduce her reading load. And she'd be reading her lectures off the same notes she made for last semester, because it wouldn't really matter whether students were listening to her or not. So now, in that least-effort scenario (which would probably result in terrible teaching evaluations and wouldn't get her rehired), Jane might get her workload down to maybe 250 hours for the course, for an hourly rate all the way up to $14.40 an hour!

As bad as that is, a stipend of $3,600 for a three-credit course is actually on the high end of normal. The American Association of University Professors reports that the median for a three-credit course nationally is $2,700. So take everything I've said and figure three-quarters of that.

LAYERS OF INDIGNITY

A collapsing career path has outcomes far beyond the financial. Contingent life wears people down in many, many ways.

First, a contingent researcher or teacher has no right to speak her or his mind. Intellectual freedom, the basis of academic life, lies far in the future, if at all. Candace, a postdoc at a research university, spoke about the ways in which she and her colleagues are silenced.

> I mean people call postdocs a special kind of hell, but the biggest issue here is bosses who are bullies. I've worked with dumb people or clueless people before, but here, we get this verbal harassment, get talked down to—always a condescending tone. They assume we have no skills; we literally get handed low-end tasks because

"the postdocs have nothing better to do." I mean, when I make recommendations about the grant, things that I think would be really
helpful for students, my boss is happy to remind me that she could
make my position part-time and I'd lose my benefits. They joke
about how a postdoc is a form of institutionalized slavery; that kind
of perceived humor is normal.

In my graduate department, I really felt like I was a part of the
community, teaching and mentoring. Here, they treat postdocs like
we're leeches, like we just take take take and we're going to walk
away with all these resources. You know, we're bringing some resources, too. . . . And the grant is just so focused on hierarchy. When
the team is introduced, the team leaders are always introduced with
"Doctor." But the postdocs never are. And I'm like, "I'm a doctor,
too. . . ."

But Candace's career depends now almost entirely on strong recommendations from her postdoctoral supervisors, so the daily hu-
miliations must stand in the faint hope that someday, faithful service
will be rewarded.

A similar story of self-censorship from Annette, an adjunct faculty member at a big university, with a doctorate from an elite research school and nearly forty years of teaching experience:

One big problem with the contingent system is that people in these
positions consider the prestige to be part of their compensation.
There's a dynamic akin to "passing," in which students don't know
the difference, call you "professor." There's a lot more support and
respect from students than the invisibility you have from the institution. The lure of respect and deference from students means it's
harder to be public, to expose yourself as an exploited worker.

If Annette wants to come back for another semester, she knows
that discretion about her circumstances is part of the price of renewal.
Sometimes discretion must be held about more than just dis-
respect. A crowdsourced document on sexual harassment in the

academy asks respondents to identify their own positions at the time of the events.[7] The vast majority of the nearly three thousand respondents were undergraduate students, graduate students, post-docs, and adjunct or visiting faculty—those supervised by persons in power over their academic futures. Direct confrontation, or re-porting up the chain, can lead to immediate withdrawal of any sup-port, or to active undermining of one's reputation and prospects among colleagues. Safer to stay silent.

So bad pay, no benefits, *and* silencing. But wait, there's more! There's also no job security. The news carries stories of factory and store closures that lay off hundreds or thousands of employees at once, a termination that always comes as a terrific shock to the workers. Higher ed carries no such surprise: academia essentially lays off all of its contingent employees at the end of each contract. Even someone who does terrific work over and over for a decade, someone whose work is valued and desired by her college, has to wonder until the first day of class every semester whether her next job will come through. Here's Eleanor, who's taught between two and four courses most semesters at the same school for eleven years:

> Typically I'll be asked about a month prior to the end of semester to teach the next semester's courses. However, until registration is over, whenever that falls, I'm never sure if all the courses will hap-pen. Sometimes there are not enough students signed up, so the course is canceled; sometimes a course gets eliminated from the curriculum. . . . I've lost courses right at the beginning of the semes-ter because of low enrollment, or because they combined two sec-tions into one. It's always a possibility, so you can't truly expect to have the teaching be a reliable source of income.

OK, so bad pay, no benefits, silencing, *and* the constant worry that next semester might not even be as financially viable as this one. But beyond all that, there is always, always, the promise that brings everyone back: the promise that if they do this assignment well, there'll be a place at the master's table someday.

Rebecca, for instance, has been an adjunct at a research university for thirteen years. She thought it would be a step toward a faculty career.

> When I took the job at [research university], I totally had a foot-in-the-door mindset. After a few years I was a finalist for a full-time non-tenure-track position in my department, and I discovered by accident that one of my colleagues was also a finalist, and she'd been with the school for twenty-five years. I had this real panic; our family very much needs the money, I had a strong interest in this position, but I thought it was completely unfair that I might get the position instead of her. I agonized over what I'd do if I were offered the position. As it turns out, neither one of us got it. The whole experience was unsettling; it was disillusioning, left a sour taste in my mouth.

Paul, an adjunct for ten years, has been a finalist for three different positions at the school he works for, as well as at least two others. He's seen jobs change from permanent to contingent even in the process of filling them:

> The landscape of being allowed in changed. Positions disappeared during the hiring process, or became fake—they'd hire someone off the page, not connected to their job description. As a program is trying to figure out what it is, trying to get uppity, they're advertising to see who they're going to get. If they get the "right" candidate, the one who makes the program look better, they'll take that person regardless of the original job description.
>
> Positions that were intended as permanent became one-year with possible renewal. They'd be advertised as tenure-track, but mysteriously become year-to-year during the process.

So here we are. Bad pay, no benefits, silencing, semester-to-semester job insecurity, and bad-faith promises that keep everyone on edge, like the dog whose master pretends to throw the ball. This is the fate that awaits the majority of the most well educated workforce in our nation. And these are the teachers who await the majority of our students.

TIERS OF TEACHING

Niccole's assertion notwithstanding, though, the system *isn't* coming to a crash. Our reliance on adjunct faculty isn't an accident; it's a standard operating feature of a system of higher education designed to offer vastly different tiers of service to vastly different populations of privilege. Dinner for two could range from $1,500 at Masa in New York City, to $150 at Hen of the Wood here in Vermont, to $15 at Taco Bell everywhere, but at least we're clear about what we're getting when we make our reservation (or pull up at the drive-through). The consumer environment of college likewise steers a vast number of students into multiple service levels, but without ever being explicit about exactly what's being purchased, or why some receive elite attention while others are waited on by minimum-wage temps. Not surprisingly, the fates of the teaching and learning communities are interwoven: the least privileged students are likely to have the least privileged teachers. The gutting of the faculty is happening fastest at the bottom, among the students and families who are least likely to notice, and least empowered to resist.

And everybody involved in the business knows that. One student services director at a second-tier state college, a school that employs about two-thirds adjunct faculty, told me, "We're doing college visits right now with our daughter. She's a good student; our school really wouldn't be right for her."

The Walmart heirs needn't buy the merchandise sold at the stores that made them wealthy, and those involved in operating the colleges of the working and middle classes often purchase their own children a product from a higher-tier establishment as well. The son of a good friend who has spent her career as a faculty member and then provost of a private college with 40 percent part-time faculty, and who is now president of a college with 60 percent part-timers, has chosen one of the nation's elite liberal arts colleges, a school where a mere 15 percent of faculty are part-time. The son of another close friend who directs an academic program at a modest state college with 55 percent part-timers went only to major research universities for his college visits—and as I listened to his mother describe the preparations for his choice, I was struck to hear words my parents never would have spoken when I was choosing a school for myself forty years ago:

- "Let's think about which of these schools would be a good fit for you."
- "I know the tuition is high, but I'm sure they have financial aid."
- "I'll take a week in March and we can go visit some schools."
- "Let me talk with the registrar and see if I can get this straightened out."
- "You should see who the faculty are in your department; you might be able to do some research with them."
- "They have a summer orientation week in July for incoming freshmen; you'll enjoy that."
- "We'll get you a new laptop before you go."

These aren't surprising words; millions of parents are saying something similar right now. But millions of other parents can't take a week from work to do campus visits. They can't pay for another unsupported week of travel for summer orientation, they don't have the understanding of college structures that would allow them to intervene, and they wouldn't know how to evaluate one school or one program against another. Cultural capital accrues across generations, and a lot of our students, as bright and eager as they may be, are starting without much in the account. They'll be the ones met at the gates by the least supported faculty, those with the fewest connections to move them further down the road.

CRIMES WITHOUT CRIMINALS

Here's the biggest problem. Although these stories of adjunct life are appalling, there is no villain. The "combat narratives" of teachers beset by evil administrators or cavalier state legislatures will not hold under close examination. No, it's worse than that.

> What *is* our primary obligation? How do we make the best experience we can with the resources we have? There are endless ways to spend on educational quality . . . how do we choose from among them and have restraint? You have to know what it is you'll trade, and what you won't. If I've only got eighty students on a floor of the dorms instead of one hundred, I'm still going to have RAs. I'm going to have financial aid, going to have a library. In the face of enrollment fluidity, what's the most scalable part of the enterprise? Classrooms. — Terry, VP for planning at a small private college

The contingency of higher education, the willingness to settle for less in the one area that matters most, is the outcome of a vast shift in our beliefs about who should go to college, and what kinds of experiences they should expect to find there. It is the outcome of millions of well-intentioned decisions that have led to tragically unintended consequences for students and teachers alike. College, especially college designed for those less than elite, is profoundly contingent. It's contingent upon enrollment, contingent upon funding shifts, contingent upon consumer demand, contingent upon national educational and employment trends. The surprise isn't that the majority of faculty are now also contingent; the surprise is that there are any permanent faculty left at all.

The function of this book is to demonstrate the ways in which both students and potential faculty members are tracked into these tiers of service, and what each tier offers by way of career and life opportunities. It is a way of helping families of pending undergraduates know what they're getting into, and who will lead their intellectual growth. It's a way of understanding why our colleges' priorities have shifted away from hiring faculty, and toward the purchase of other resources. And it's a way of helping graduate students understand whether their advanced degrees will be the key to meaningful faculty careers.

This is the book my family should have had when they considered sending me to college. It's the book I should have had when I considered graduate school. It's a book that grows from fundamental questions of what college is, what college teaching is, and why some participants—both students and teachers—are secure while others remain ever uncertain.

2

THE PERMANENT AND
THE CONTINGENT

Adjunct (*n*): something joined or added to another thing but not essentially a part of it.
— Merriam-Webster Dictionary online

Every institution has its hierarchy, the ranking system that distinguishes enlisted from officer, duke from viscount, priest from bishop. College and university faculty — the body of scholars whose primary job is to design and create classroom instruction, academic research, and intellectual guidance for individual students — are no different.

The fundamental distinction in faculty life, its two major communities, are commonly known as tenure-track (TT) and non-tenure-track (NTT). Tenure-track faculty — the people we think of when we're asked to consider the idea of "college professor" — are hired with the intention of permanence. They teach and engage in scholarly life; they set the course of the curricula within their departments and set the core curricula for the entire college. The TT faculty are entrusted with the enduring intellectual life of the school; their interests become the college's interests, and their intellectual curiosity creates areas of academic strength and research centers within the larger landscape. They receive significant investment in their ongoing development, with professional memberships, conference travel, research equipment, and information resources available to them, and with paid sabbaticals offered for the development of particularly promising research. The easy focus is on the blunt fact of tenure, the assurance of employment after a probationary period; but more importantly, TT designation means that the institution cares about them enough to invest in their professional growth, and trusts them enough to give them the keys to curricular design and research autonomy.

There is a second order of the faculty class, though, for whom such investment and trust do not exist for any reason or in any form: the non-tenure-track or NTT faculty. They differ from the TT in several ways. There is no expectation of permanence; indeed, the expectation is for impermanence, for contracts lasting from one course in one semester to a few years at most. NTT faculty do not set curricula, and may not even set the syllabus for their own courses, instead delivering a standard package designed by others. They are not supported to teach and do research, but instead do one or the other exclusively. They typically get little or no professional development, nor are they supported for conference travel, professional memberships, or publication expenses.

The salaries for the two communities are wildly dissimilar. The initial TT rank, assistant professor, carries a national average salary of $69,206, along with benefits packages and funding for travel and research that can account for an additional 50 percent of economic value.[1] The next higher rank, achieved after a six-year probationary period, is associate professor. The national average there is about ten thousand dollars higher, plus the status of tenure, a guarantee of lifetime employment except in cases of truly egregious or criminal misbehavior. And finally, after years of service deemed to have been excellent by one's peers, there is the full professor, averaging $102,402. Although that salary is a significant step down from that of attorneys (average $120,000) or family practice physicians ($190,000), academia has always provided a comfortable profession for its permanent members.

The NTT faculty don't fare nearly as well, ranging from the full-time postdoctoral researcher making ten or twenty thousand dollars a year less than a beginning faculty member at the same school, all the way down to the adjunct making two or three thousand dollars per course. In 2012, the Coalition on the Academic Workforce found the national average adjunct instructor stipend for a three-credit college course was about $2,700.[2] Let's assume it's gone up a little since then. Even so, those adjuncts lucky enough to put together a heavy load of courses each semester and another two in the summer (and, like Helen, driving back and forth five hundred miles a week), would be making about $30,000 a year, working far more than forty hours a week on planning and grading and student email contact, with no institutional contribution to their health care or their retirement plans, no protection for individual illness or family emergencies, and no security beyond the end of each semester. The undergraduate students they lead will themselves do far better, averaging roughly $50,000 per year straight from school.[3]

The NTTs are everywhere, but are camouflaged to look exactly like their TT counterparts in daily life. A student in a classroom, a parent sending her child into that classroom, or a professional observer would have no way of discerning whether a particular teacher was a member of one group or the other. Many NTTs are extraordinary teachers; providing a strong undergraduate classroom education is their primary job. What they *can't* provide is the larger value of collegiate life: the ongoing, year-after-year mentorship of a particularly engaged student, the easy availability between classes, the office hours where classroom material is distilled from the roiling reservoir of information into drop after drop of wisdom. What they *can't* provide, having little or no access to teaching at the doctoral level, is a voice in shaping the next generation of scholars. What they *can't* provide is a substantial contribution to the larger academic discourse within which they were trained. NTTs are content providers accomplishing a constrained task. The larger academic life of the institution is off-limits to them.

LIES, DAMN LIES . . .

More than one million people are now working as contingent faculty and instructors at U.S. institutions of higher education, providing a cheap labor source even while students' tuition has skyrocketed. Traditionally, adjuncts were experienced professionals who were still working in or recently retired from their industry outside of academia, with time on their hands to teach a class or two at the university or community college. Adjunct work supplemented their income; teaching was not their main job. Such adjuncts still exist. But national trends indicate that schools are increasingly relying on adjuncts and other contingent faculty members, rather than full-time, tenure-track professors, to do the bulk of the work of educating students. Today, being a part-time adjunct at several schools is the way many instructors cobble together full-time employment in higher education.

—Democratic staff, US House of Representatives, 2014[4]

Regardless of a great number of attempts to do so, it's almost impossible to count how many college teachers are tenure-track and how many are contingent. The terms in use vary from one school to another, from one oversight system to another, from one watchdog to another.

According to the American Association of University Professors, the proportion of TT college faculty permanently affiliated with their schools has fallen from about 45 percent in 1976 to about 25 percent today.[5] Another 15 to 20 percent of teachers both then and now are graduate students, learning their trade before going out onto the dangerous seas. This means that a majority of people teaching in America's colleges are now contract workers of one form or another.

The US Department of Education's Integrated Postsecondary Education Data System (IPEDS) uses a different accounting system that doesn't rely on TT and NTT, but instead designates *full-time* and *part-time* faculty. You can read the numbers yourself for what-

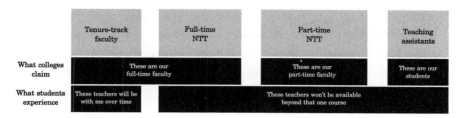

Tenure-track faculty	Full-time NTT	Part-time NTT	Teaching assistants

What colleges claim	These are our full-time faculty	These are our part-time faculty	These are our students
What students experience	These teachers will be with me over time	These teachers won't be available beyond that one course	

FIGURE 1. Gaming the numbers in reporting contingent faculty

ever school you're interested in.[6] Here in southwestern Vermont, for example, nearby Castleton University has 94 full-time and 166 part-time faculty. Green Mountain College has 39 full-time and 23 part-time. The College of St. Joseph, 10 and 34. The Community College of Vermont has zero and 611. (You read that right . . . 611 faculty members, with exactly none of them full-time.)

Since 1970, the number of students enrolled in America's colleges and universities has more than doubled, from 8.6 million to about 20 million.[7] The number of full-time faculty has roughly kept pace, from 370,000 to 790,000. The number of part-time faculty, on the other hand, has increased sevenfold, from 105,000 to 755,000.[8]

But as bad as those numbers look, it's actually worse. We often talk across one another when we refer to the number of contingent faculty, because a full-time faculty member is not the same thing as a tenure-track faculty member. Nationwide, data collected by the *Chronicle of Higher Education* shows more than half of the full-timers are themselves impermanent, hired for limited terms with no expectation of renewal, not welcomed into the larger conversations of institutional mission.[9] The American Association of University Professors shows a different proportion, with about a third of full-timers being NTT.[10] Either way, colleges have a large block of faculty who live in a middle ground of contingency, a community claimed as members when the institution wants to look good to accreditors and renounced when it comes time to grant them the privileges of TT life (see figure 1).

In principle, *student-faculty ratio* should also be pretty simple: total undergrads divided by total faculty. But what do we mean by total faculty? Only the relatively small number of tenure-track faculty? Not likely. Some professional accrediting bodies, and the federal IPEDS reporting system, define the faculty count as *full time + [part time ÷ 3]*, with each contingent teacher counting as a third of a person, academia's own version of the Three-Fifths Compromise.[11] In classroom terms, a college might indeed have a comfortable student/faculty ratio of, say, twelve to one. But take the contingent faculty out, and there are actually closer to forty or fifty students per *permanent* faculty member, making advising less frequent and less personal, and reducing students' opportunities to build the enduring relationships that will change their lives.

It's not even clear what an individual school means when it talks about its percentage of part-timers. Let's create a simple example: a middling state school with a hundred full-time and a hundred part-time faculty. The full-time faculty each teach four courses per semester, whereas the part-timers average two courses each. But the part-timers teach bigger introductory courses, averaging forty students each, whereas the full-timers are more frequently used in seminars for juniors and seniors in their major, and average fifteen students each. Table 1 shows three different ways to talk about the percentages of the same school.

Whether we're talking about an individual school or a national data set, the "percentage of adjuncts" can mean a lot of things, none of which tell us about a student's experience. It's left to prospective students and their parents to make sure that they define the local terms and practices, and understand the local arithmetic. And comparison across colleges becomes all the more opaque.

BLINDED BY LARGE NUMBERS

But, you know . . . six hundred thousand, a million, 70 percent, blah blah blah. When we get into these giant numbers, people's eyes glaze over. To quote Joseph Stalin, the death of an individual is a tragedy, but the death of a million is a statistic. So let's go smaller, see how this all plays out at an aerial view of one school. Here's a description

TABLE 1   One college, three percentages

FT faculty count	100
PT faculty count	100
Total faculty	200
Percentage of PT faculty	50% (100 PT out of 200)
FT sections taught	800 (100 faculty at 8 courses per year)
PT sections taught	400 (100 faculty at 4 courses per year)
Total sections	1200
Percentage of courses taught by PT faculty	33% (400 taught by PT out of 1,200 total)
FT students taught	12,000 (800 sections at 15 students each)
PT students taught	16,000 (400 sections at 40 students each)
Total student seats	28,000
Percentage of students taught by PT faculty	57% (16,000 taught by PT out of 28,000 total)

of a writing program at a giant public research university, responsible for an array of writing courses that enroll more than seventeen
thousand students each year.

> The writing program teaches nine hundred courses a year. It's
> staffed by a hundred PTLs, a hundred and twenty TAs, thirty full-
> time NTTs, and one tenured faculty member who's the director.
> —Annette, forty-year adjunct

This blur of abbreviations and roles is invisible to most students
and families, who look on their course schedules and see a name,
and who come to the classroom to be taught by a person. However,
our idea of a college faculty member, the tenured professor, is represented in this writing program by one single person, whose TT
position offers stable membership within the university. The other
250 are something else.

Within the NTT community, this particular writing program has
two smaller groups. This school uses the term "PTL" to denote a
part-time lecturer: the scavenger, the bottom feeder, paid by the

course as need arises. The PTLs are sufficiently qualified to teach their specific courses—freshman composition, business writing, or the like. Many, like Annette, have been trained as scholars, with PhDs and snuffed career aspirations as academics. The university claims no ongoing responsibility for them, allowing their numbers to rise and fall as enrollment dictates. The hundred of them account for the teaching of at least a third and perhaps as many as a half of the nine hundred courses, each PTL taking on one or two courses per semester.

The "full-time NTT" is a neither-nor, although schools love to tout the *full-time* part of that formulation, hoping that the civilians won't notice that they're not really members of the TT order. They probably make a marginally livable wage—twenty or thirty thousand dollars less than a starting assistant professor—and they might have the benefits package and maybe even a retirement plan contribution. But their contract is for a fixed term, most often three to five years, after which their services are no longer required. And just as a finch can never become a hawk, members of the NTT order almost never morph into TT. They are a lesser order of life, well down the food chain, unwelcomed and unsupported once their utility has been depleted.

Although the full-time NTT have little say in the design of courses or the larger curricula within which they fit, they are often given some administrative work to do (in exchange for a twelve-month contract, meaning that their summers are no longer available for the research and writing they might otherwise have taken up as part of their career development). They might schedule and supervise the tutoring center, play a role in program assessment, or play a role in hiring and coordinating and reviewing the work of the lowest caste of PTL scavengers. All of this leaves the TT faculty—remember him, that one guy who runs the thing?—free to write journal articles, travel to conferences, and present himself as the public face of the project, borrowing glory from the labor of the unseen.

And then there is the largest group of all in this case: the teaching assistant, or TA. One might think that, as the name implies, teaching assistants assist teachers, leading discussion groups and taking attendance and grading papers. But very often, as in this case, TAs are moderately advanced graduate students who are given classrooms of their own, supplied with only the readings and the roster, and told to get to work. The TAs, holding steady at between 15 and 20 percent of the collegiate teaching force, are fundamentally students, working on the development of their own scholarly lives. Their teaching-assistantship is the bargain they make with the university, paying their tuition by teaching a course each semester. Although they teach, they are not faculty. They are part of a different community, the students. They are akin to the amphibians in this ecosystem, adapting as needed to both the student and teacher environments.

So when we look at the actual service provided, those nine hundred courses each year, it probably breaks down something like this:

- TA: 240 courses (120 people teaching one course per semester)
- Full-time NTT: 180 courses (30 people teaching three courses per semester)
- PTL: all the rest, about 480 courses (100 PTLs teaching one to three courses per semester)
- TT faculty: 2 courses (one person teaching one course per semester, with the rest of the salary earned as program director)

Put another way, your daughter attending this high-powered, well-endowed, exclusive university is roughly 99.8 percent likely to take first-year writing from a teacher only temporarily and provisionally affiliated with the school.

Writing programs are often among the worst examples of the imbalanced ecosystem, along with lower-division math courses, science-for-nonmajors courses, first- and second-semester world languages, and introductory social science and humanities courses. We'll talk later about why these microclimates are particularly toxic for the teaching population, but for the moment, notice one thing: they constitute a significant component of the first-year student's experience. As long ago as the year 2000, the Association for Institutional Research found that at one relatively typical public university, approximately 80 percent of all first-year students had three or more of their first-semester courses taught by part-time faculty; they also found a correlation between exposure to part-time faculty and a decision to not return for a second semester.[12] These freshmen—these newcomers to academic life, young people making fundamental decisions about whether or not the enterprise is worth their while—are being greeted at the door by the most tenuous, least affiliated members of the community.

This may not be wise.

The contingency of the first-year experience helps to explain why a quarter of US freshmen don't become sophomores; and why, for the schools most reliant on adjuncts, that 25 percent is closer to 40 percent.[13] The classroom experiences, each taken on its own, may be fine, but the larger collegiate experience of systemic entry into intellectual adulthood is lost.

UNSPOKEN BELIEFS AND THEIR UNSEEN OUTCOMES

To even use a phrase like "the larger collegiate experience of systemic entry into intellectual adulthood" is to tip my hand, to state the mission of higher education in a way that makes clear what is being lost by the contemporary reliance on contingency. This is not the language used by others to describe their interests in higher ed.

For example, some might offer explicit acknowledgement of career training . . .

> Prepare for your rewarding career at Gavilan College and obtain an education that reflects the needs of the community and anticipates changes in demands in business and industry. The Career and Technical Education department provides students with the skills and opportunities necessary to survive and thrive in today's competitive business world. Students completing CTE programs at Gavilan are

in high demand in the job market and are better able to provide for their families and themselves.[14]

... or the importance of research ...

Each year, the UC Berkeley campus receives well over half a billion dollars in research and other support from external sources. In the fiscal year ending June 30, 2017, UC Berkeley attracted $847.5 million in new awards.[15]

... or of just having postadolescent fun:

There's just something about Duke sports. Even if you're not a dedicated sports fan, it's tough to resist the infectious fun that exists at Duke, as when the main university quad fills with blue-painted students cheering around a bonfire after a big win. There's a real camaraderie and an incredible sense of spirit—and running around a bonfire after a huge win with your face painted blue along with everyone you know is something you'll only experience at Duke.[16]

Higher education in America is pulled in dozens of competing directions at once: as a research core, as a job-training center, as a minor-league professional sports franchise, as a nurturer of citizens, as a business magnet, as a real-estate developer, as a major regional employer, as an extended-adolescence day care center. These competing beliefs about higher education have provided the churning environment within which contingency has thrived. As Yogi Berra once said, "If you don't know where you're goin', you'll wind up somewhere else." If we don't know our core goals for college—individually or culturally—then we can't be clear about the student-faculty relations that will get us there.

3

BRONZE, SILVER, GOLD, OR PLATINUM

The assumption that "a college degree" means something without the college's being specified is woven so deeply into the American myth that it
dies very hard, even when confronted with the facts of the class system
and its complicity with the hierarchies of higher learning. . . . In *A Nation
of Strangers*, [Vance Packard] writes cheerfully, "In 1940, about 13 percent
of college-age young people actually went to college; by 1970 it was about
43 percent." But no. It was still about 13 percent, with the other 30 percent
attending things merely denominated colleges. These poor kids and their
parents were performing the perpetual American quest not for intellect
but for respectability and status.
  — Paul Fussell, *Class*

Paul Fussell, a combination of scholar (PhD from Harvard, history
faculty at Connecticut College, then Rutgers, and finally Penn) and
gadfly, wrote these words in the early 1980s. Now, thirty-five years
later, the proportion of high school graduates moving directly into
college has risen to nearly 70 percent. The scale of the higher education enterprise has doubled since the publication of Fussell's book,
but the basic facts have not. Much more recently, Stanford education professor David Labaree wrote the following in his history of
American higher education:

. . . Stratification is at the heart of American education. It's the price we pay for the system's broad accessibility. We let everyone in, but they all get a different experience, and they all win different social benefits from those experiences. In this way the system is both strongly populist and strongly elitist, allowing ordinary people a high possibility of getting ahead through education and a low probability of getting ahead very far.[1]

It's easy, and all too American, to focus on some perceived scalar rank of individual colleges, the kind of "my school is better than your school" nonsense that results in the annual *US News and World Report* college rankings, and in brawls after hockey games. What I'd like to do instead in this chapter is to acknowledge that there are different tiers of schools that have entirely different definitions of college and of college outcomes. They support different communities of students who come with different privileges and different goals. And they employ radically different faculty to conduct their work.

JEAN ANYON AND THE HIDDEN CURRICULUM

Every scholar has his or her *ur*-sources, the handful of articles or books that changed their thinking and illuminated a new world. One of mine is "Social Class and the Hidden Curriculum of Work," by the late Jean Anyon, an education scholar first at Rutgers and later at the City University of New York.[2] It's a brilliantly simple piece of work: Anyon and her research team spent time observing five elementary schools in a single district in northern New Jersey, watching what fifth grade teachers said and did, watching what fifth graders themselves said and did.

Her work was informed by interests in social class, and so the schools she selected for observation were spread across that array. Two schools were working-class, with parents of tenuous working conditions: barmaids, foundry workers, security guards. A third was middle-class, with parents who were skilled technical workers: contractors, tradesmen, nurses, teachers, firefighters. A fourth was home to what she called "affluent professional" families, the kids of lawyers and engineers, of designers and ad men. And the final school was that of the one percent: executives, corporate counsel, financiers.

What she found was striking. In every case, the schools used similar curricular materials to teach their fifth-graders similar subjects. But the day-to-day facts of life, what she called the "hidden curriculum," were entirely unlike one another. In every case, schools were training students to become their parents, to take on ways of thinking and acting that would mirror their eventual social class and working lives.

- In the working-class schools, the primary lesson, regardless of subject, was obedience and procedure. Copy the steps, copy the notes, fill in the form, color the picture. "Sit down." "Shut up." "Where's your book?" "Why are you out of your seat?"
- In the middle-class schools, the lesson was learning or calculating the right answer. Pop quiz, punctuation worksheets, store the facts until needed later. "That's correct." "Read it again." "Look it up."
- In the professional school, the lesson was creative expression, both independent and collaborative. Design the page, imagine the process, write the essay, paint the mural. "That's beautiful!" "Check with what your neighbor has done." "Are you satisfied with that paragraph now?"
- In the executive school, the lesson was analytical and strategic. See the pattern, develop the work plan, find the flaw, present your work with authority. "Don't be afraid to say if you disagree." "What mistakes did Pericles make after the war?" "Reason it through." "What's your first decision with this kind of problem?"

In each of these schools, the formal curricula would have shown as the same subjects: arithmetic and social studies, language arts and science. But the underlying intentions were worlds apart. And those unspoken messages—about the characteristics of a smart person, about individual versus collective success, about the benefits of initiative and creativity and judgment—weigh more than the contents of the courses.

Colleges begin from that hierarchy and refine the gradients even more strongly, by both selectivity and delivery. Just as in Anyon's analysis, there are a few primary types of colleges that collectively educate most of America's undergraduates, each with its own faculty population. Students can take calculus and composition at all of them, but the underlying intentions and the resulting daily experiences reach for entirely different outcomes.

CONVENIENCE AND LOW PRICE FOR THE WORKING CLASS

The analogues to the "working-class" school are the two-year or community colleges, accounting for about 25 percent of all institutions and about 40 percent of all undergrad enrollment.[3] Many of these students have no family history of education; 52 percent of first-generation students choose community colleges, as opposed to only 28 percent of students with at least one college-educated parent.[4] These are the students who didn't grow up with books and magazines around the house, whose parents didn't have a week in March to take them on college tours and wouldn't have had the confidence or the awareness of whom to call at a university to straighten out a misunderstanding. These young people are sent by family members who may have felt demeaned by their own experiences in school, and who may have mixed feelings about their children's participation in it.

Community colleges rarely have a residential component; they primarily serve a "community" or tightly regional population of students who commute to school. Many traditional-aged students live at home, their room and board absorbed within normal family operations. Many more are nontraditional students, adults already engaged in family and working lives.[5] Over 20 percent of women students in community colleges are single mothers.[6] As a result, community colleges have a substantially larger part-time student population than other kinds of schools, as students fit coursework into already demanding schedules.

Community colleges have diverse missions: they aim at getting their students transferred into four-year schools; at vocational and technical study for certification in the trades; and at broad community outreach, with programming both recreational (yoga, piano) and social (English as a second language, parenting skills).[7] Community college can be where you go to get your calculus and intro psych taken care of inexpensively; it can also be where you go to get training to become a welder or paralegal or baker, or to go to the gym more cheaply than any health-club membership.

Because of their other commitments and often tenuous economic status, adult students with jobs and families find it impossible to shop nationally or even regionally for a college, leaving them a much more limited array of local schools from which to choose.[8] So two of the main (and competing) draws of community colleges are cost and convenience. They are the least expensive option in higher ed, with a national average full-time tuition of about $3,500.[9] But in their efforts to "meet students where they are," community colleges paradoxically have to be more responsive to more needs than do their four-year peers. Schools have to jump quickly onto employment needs in their region, while also having to develop "articulation agreements" or systems of curricular alignment with numerous four-year schools so that their students can transfer more easily and successfully. They have to support full-time students who can take four or five courses a semester, and accommodate others who can only take one course at a time, or who have to skip a semester to earn enough money for the next.

They have to offer more courses at multiple times of day to fit varying work schedules. Bunker Hill Community College in Boston led the nation in offering graveyard-shift courses, an array of common requirements taught from 11:30 p.m. to 2:30 a.m. to meet the needs of working parents who'd finally put their kids to bed, or bartenders just off shift from TGI Fridays.[10] They face similar pressure to compress three class sessions each week into a single weekly three-hour chunk that exhausts everyone's attention, and even greater pressure to just put the whole thing online so that overwhelmed students can do it all from home, or on their smartphones while they're on the bus to work.[11]

Community colleges are most often "open-admission" or entirely unselective. Over 50 percent of entering students require at least one remedial course, and often many more. In California, the nation's largest community college system, which enrolls a fifth of all CC students nationwide, nearly 80 percent of incoming students require remedial work, which slows or stalls their progress toward transfer or certification.[12] Because so many students are underprepared and have so little personal or family experience with educational possibilities, there's a strong impulse to minimize confusion and false starts through "guided pathways" or strictly constrained curricular sequences that give students clear steps on the floor to be followed.[13] (Remember Jean Anyon's working-class fifth grade? Obedience and procedure.) Advising is a matter of simply following instructions, working students down a checklist of courses that aims at their pre-planned destination.

The fast-food demands that community colleges face—the demand for low cost to serve an economically tenuous community, the demand for convenience in the form of innumerable time slots, the demand for remedial classes, and the existence of a large body of students unable to get into more serious academic environments—have led to a fast-food employment structure in which almost three-quarters of community college faculty are adjunct.[14] And these adjuncts are the worst paid of all, with stipends hovering around $2,500 per three-credit course.[15] The students with the least cultural capital and the least prior educational success are provided with the teachers who are lowest paid, least secure, and least informed about or connected to campus initiatives designed to help struggling students.

As a result, community college is fundamentally an individual, course-by-course experience for both faculty and students. There is little opportunity for a larger collegiate life, and no reliable cohort to offer mutual support and encouragement in tough moments. Everyone is a free agent, a solo producer or consumer of credits and certification, trying to scrape their way into economic security. The teacher in front of a community college precalculus class may be a stellar instructor, but she is hobbled at every turn as she makes her way through the course, and she will have no deeper relationship with her students between classes or in semesters to come.

We see the outcomes. Only 60 percent of community college freshmen become community college sophomores.[16] Only 15 percent ultimately achieve a bachelor's degree.[17] For those 15 percent, community college offers an invaluable first step toward an otherwise unattainable future, a restart button that allows them to rise above the fate of their families. For the rest—and for their teachers—it's deeply uncertain what's been gained, and what the convenience has cost.

THE COMFORTABLE GENERALIST AND THE MIDDLE-CLASS COLLEGE

The "middle-class" colleges are the state comprehensive schools, the Central Michigans and West Texas A&Ms and Chico States around the country. These schools reflect their origins as technical colleges and normal schools that provided skilled workers for a regional economy. Most states have an identifiable tier system of higher education, in which the flagship research universities are clearly differentiated from the lesser "comprehensive" schools that serve far-flung communities. Sometimes the regional comprehensives are operated as a network of schools separate from the research universities: California has the University of California system of research universities, and a separate Cal State system of regional four-year schools, Vermont has the University of Vermont and then the Vermont State Colleges. Often, though, they're nominally part of the same system while knowing that their betters at the big schools will never acknowledge them. Say "University of North Carolina" to someone and they'll tell you about Chapel Hill, not UNC-Pembroke; "University of Wisconsin" evokes Madison, not Platteville.

Nonetheless, these regional colleges and universities are full four-year schools, increasingly offering master's and occasionally even doctoral degrees as they strive for respect just as their students do. To be fair, they're also moving toward graduate programs in recognition that an undergraduate degree is increasingly commonplace, and as a business strategy in pursuit of making more money from the demographic bulge that recently graduated from college during the late 2000s. Just between 2010 and 2015, ninety-four previously baccalaureate colleges shifted into the master's camp, increasing the master's category by about 15 percent.[18] In Massachusetts, all state colleges became state universities in 2010. In 2015, Vermont's Castleton State College abandoned "State" altogether, deeming itself to be Castleton University.

These schools serve moderately larger geographic regions, and thus usually have housing and dining services, though there are still lots of commuters. Increasingly, as schools seek new revenue sources, they work to recruit out-of-state and international students, who pay tuition two and three times the in-state rate. These schools offer degrees in many of the historic academic disciplines, but also work to provide the skilled vocations to which many first-generation students and their families aspire: nursing and health science, athletic training and exercise science, sports administration, criminal justice, and hospitality management. These are degrees you can take to the HR departments of your local hospital, ski resort, conference hotel, or police academy, and start your career a few steps above the entry level.

The permanent teachers at these schools will mostly have doctorates or profession-specific terminal master's degrees like MBAs and MFAs, and the schools will have recruited those faculty through national searches. But they still rely strongly on adjuncts to do their teaching. Public colleges that offer only bachelor's degrees employ about 62 percent contingent faculty; even those that offer master's degrees are still 56 percent adjunct.[19] And though places like Boston and San Francisco are lousy with PhDs, the far-flung towns that are home to regional schools have a tougher time finding local people with doctoral degrees. The accreditors' definitions of "qualified faculty" usually include possession of a degree higher than the one that a course's students aspire to, so teachers with master's degrees make up a sizeable population of both the TT and NTT populations for baccalaureate courses.[20] In rural areas, even master's degrees are relatively uncommon for local residents, and lower-level courses might be taught by adjuncts with bachelor's degrees and some professional experience. Having more content knowledge than one's students is the fundamental qualification.

It's also at the regional comprehensives that I first encountered a different category of adjunct altogether: a sizeable number of people already employed by the college in some other capacity. They work for their colleges in different roles: as directors of tutoring, athletic department trainers, librarians, webmasters, and online marketing directors. They teach a class every semester to pick up a little extra money for a retirement or vacation fund, for child care, or to make up for missing child support payments from their exes. The extra money makes a difference at Christmas and birthdays. This invisible adjunct population, almost none of whom have doctorates, are inherently part of the collegiate support staff, but are easy to tap because they're close at hand and already in the payroll system.

Have a look at the staff directory of any middling state college, and you'll find them. Here are a few at one nearby school:

- head athletic trainer, part-time faculty
- IT technician, part-time faculty
- comptroller, part-time faculty
- strength and conditioning coach, part-time faculty
- coordinator of disability services, part-time faculty

- associate registrar, part-time faculty
- director of digital media, part-time faculty
- dean of advancement, part-time faculty

Another body of part-time faculty at the regional schools, in an unexpected way, is the TT faculty itself, especially in teaching-intensive schools without strong research expectations. Lots of community colleges and lower-tier four-year schools have an un-spoken reliance on "overload assignments," in which tenured fac-ulty members expected to teach four courses per semester actually teach five or six, plus a couple more in the summer, usually at ad-junct piecework rates in order to augment their salary. This is at least better for students than having a baseball coach pick up that course; these are faculty who understand the discipline and the entirety of the curriculum, and who can act as longer-term mentors. But it's still just another second job that augments the insufficiency of the first, spreading faculty attention more thinly than the college encourages in its own hiring guidelines.

If the community colleges prepare students to mirror their fac-ulty's lives as isolated individuals scratching out a tenuous survival, the state comprehensives also prepare students to mirror their own faculty's lives, with secure-enough jobs that provide for the mort-gage, the golf clubs, and the new SUV every few years. They pre-pare students to become the generalists whom smaller places rely upon, where the specialist isn't as helpful as a person who can do quite a few things acceptably well, and who can fill multiple roles.[21] In a small city, any decently educated person might serve on the city council, or work weekends as a ski instructor, or occasionally teach business communications at the local college; the work needs doing even if there isn't much money for it, so someone just steps up and does it. This is the role of faculty at the middle-class school, because it's the role for which students at the middle-class school are being trained, regardless of their major.

THE MONASTERIES OF THE LIBERAL ARTS

Students begin with a first year seminar that's only taught by tenure-track faculty, capped at twelve to fifteen students. The basic methods courses are only taught by tenure-track faculty. At the other end, the capstone courses as well tend to be twelve to fifteen students. All of the core courses in the majors are only open to tenure-track faculty. Most of the real academic counseling and advising is conducted by faculty, especially as students declare a major. We want close mentoring relationships between students and faculty, and that requires permanence.

—Maura, dean of the faculty at a selective liberal arts college

The "affluent professional" schools are the highly selective liberal arts colleges, some of the unique schools of the country, places like Reed, Smith, and Oberlin. These are where broad-minded families send their bohemian offspring to design their own majors, where one's life is designed to be a limitless fount of creativity, exploration, and self-determination. These are the schools where students are expected to take charge of their own curricula and their own learning, to create unique expressions of their own intellectual and identity interests—schools where every student is carefully selected for their ability to surprise and delight and challenge the others.

Adjuncts are far less common here, employed to cover sick leaves or sabbaticals, or to teach specialized but rarely demanded skills like oboe performance or musical theater choreography. Oberlin College, for instance, has 326 full-time and 59 part-time faculty. Middlebury has 314 and 56; Bates has 156 and 37; Reed has 161 and 6; Davidson has 185 and 4.[22] These are places where the faculty are chosen not merely for content knowledge but, more importantly, for their ability to guide generations of students to independent and creative thought.

We talk too simply about "mentorship," which is far more than teaching. A real mentor reveals the pleasures and richness of a culture in ways that make it seem attainable to another. She or he provides entry to a new community, a new life, fostering connections into a web of possibility. An increasing body of literature on higher education confirms the lasting importance of close personal relationships between a student and a faculty member.[23] We are people, after all, and not merely units of production and consumption. We can be enthused and discouraged, eager and hesitant, at different moments. We need to know that others have our backs, will celebrate with us, will push us further than we thought we might be able to go on our own.

This responsibility for social support is not carried merely by the faculty. Elite liberal arts colleges are almost entirely residential, with students living side by side twenty-four hours a day, relieved from the duties of the world. They walk together like monks through the ritual days of devotion. Every incoming freshman arriving in September 2019 will be met at the door with materials proclaiming them to be a member of the Class of 2023; they are set forth together on a mutual course of known duration and unimaginable creativity. Over 90 percent of them will get there.

One of the reasons they'll survive the journey is that most of their families have the financial and emotional resources to support them. These students primarily come from comfort and security, and know they can take some chances in life and still land on their feet. They can take the unpaid summer internship at a prestigious magazine instead of a summer job painting houses. They can major in physics instead of engineering, in literature instead of digital marketing, in dance instead of athletic training. They can change majors in light of discovering some great new love, and not have their families think that they've derailed. They aren't learning a trade; they're learning the skills of analysis, enthusiasm, and creativity, the skills that will let them move into new arenas with confidence. They will become leaders rather than workers, and they're supported in that endeavor by a stable permanent faculty.

The cost, selectivity, and quirky curricula of the elite schools leads them to take very few transfer students, a fact that we will soon see as paired with the relatively low contingency of the adults around them. These are uniquely specialized ecosystems, with wildlife as specifically evolved as that of Madagascar.

These conditions do not necessarily hold, by the way, at the large flock of lesser private colleges, many of whom bear far more relation to middle-class state comprehensives, including their origins as regional professional schools (those professions most often being the ministry or Christian motherhood), their increasing shift toward master's-level and career degrees, and a substantial reliance on adjuncts. The elite liberal arts colleges share four common field markings: a full focus on undergraduate learning, a substantial endowment that provides added income, a competitive admissions process, and full-timers making up 80 percent or more of their faculty.

THE MASTERS OF THE UNIVERSE

We hire most of our new architects from two schools, [state technical college] and [top-tier research university]. The [state] kids, I can put them to work instantly; they're productive within a week. The [top-tier] kids need a lot more technical training. But after five years, the [top-tier] grads are project managers, and the [state] students are still in the back room doing production.
  —Olivia, architect

Take an elite liberal arts college, and bolt on a medical school, a law school, a business school, a pharmaceutical laboratory, a particle accelerator, some major-league sports franchises, and a multi-billion-dollar endowment. Clamp the lid down tight so that the pressure builds. Make sure that everyone knows that the expectations are intense, and that anything less than perfection is failure.

Welcome to the machine.

The "executive" schools are the nation's most highly research-focused institutions, which offer degrees from bachelors' to doctorates and often have a grad student population double the number of the undergrads. It's an exclusive club, starting with the old landscapes and old money of the Ivy League: Brown, Columbia, Cornell, Dartmouth, Harvard, Penn, Princeton, and Yale. Then add the handful of other major private research universities: NYU, Duke, Chicago, Stanford, MIT, Johns Hopkins, Caltech, USC, and such. Then the most research-focused (and football-focused) state flagship schools: Ohio State, Michigan, Minnesota, UNC, UC Berkeley, UCLA, Wisconsin, Penn State, Georgia Tech, Washington.[24] One hundred fifteen of them in total.

These are schools that aim their students at national and international lives. Gone are the degree programs in interior design and athletic management; mostly absent as well are degree programs in skilled vocations such as aviation technology and social work. These colleges are not training their students for jobs; they are training their students to rule the world.

Admission at all levels is highly competitive, and a student's opportunities can be bolstered by elite athletic performance that makes boosters happy; by a family legacy of enrollment that keeps well-to-do donors happy; or by the advancement office's discovery of family wealth that might be later tapped in donations.

Executive colleges surround students with colleagues from across the nation and around the earth, the best of the best concentrated without regard to geographic background as they learn how to navigate global diversity. Immense resources are at their disposal (as has been true during most of their younger lives as well), as they learn how to use the finest tools and the finest minds to do great things.

Here, as at the elite liberal arts colleges, success is thought to be collective rather than individual. Family support and stable faculty are a big part of that community effort, but one reason why the high-powered universities have power is that their alumni look out for the school and for one another, offering graduates entry into the higher reaches of finance and science, public service and cultural affairs.

Every school prepares its students to enter an appropriate life network, for business and friendship and marriage prospects that suit their class. The students from Yale are going to go on to be the self-proclaimed masters of the universe, to run brokerages and federal agencies, and to produce offspring even more privileged and powerful than themselves. They need to start, at age twenty, to build the community they can get on the phone fifteen years later to arrange a merger or to kick-start a piece of legislation; they need to start engaging with romantic partners who will multiply those networks, for themselves and their kids. They need to have an alumni network of older grads who've already occupied the offices that they'll be rising into. Those who go to the middle-class schools will likewise need a network, but it's going to be a different kind on a different scale. They need to know the people who will ultimately work at the HR department at the regional hospital or school district, and they need to pull a team together to organize a charity fundraiser or support a state-house candidacy. Everyone needs a professional and social network, and the sorting mechanisms of colleges determine in large part which networks their students will have access to.

At the elite universities, tenure-track faculty with PhDs are all over the place, and there are a lot of them, since the teaching load is lower in recognition of the research demands they face. Two courses per semester is the norm; one course or even none for those who are highly productive scholars with successful grant funding. The lower their teaching load, the less often they'll be seeing undergraduates, since their specialized knowledge will be focused on their specialized graduate students. This is another reason why student-faculty ratio is an unhelpful guide to college experience. A research school has tons of TT faculty, lowering the simple ratio but not class size or availability, because so little of their time is invested in undergraduate classroom education.

But that vast supply of TT faculty doesn't mean that there aren't any contingent faculty; the contingent faculty just look different. These are the schools where teaching postdocs live, for instance: fully qualified but not fully employed scholars brought in for a couple of years to teach and to help develop a focused curricular area — a first-year writing program, a minorities-in-science program, a math-across-the-curriculum program. And of course, because of the demands for research productivity, these are also the schools receiving big-money grants that employ postdoctoral researchers.

But the largest community of contingent teachers here won't be recorded in the faculty column at all: they're graduate students, at work on their own PhDs in their own research areas. As part of their training to take on a desired faculty life, graduate teaching assistants (a misnomer, since they often aren't assisting anybody, just teaching independently with only the most occasional oversight) take on one course per semester, often an introductory survey course that helps them claim a breadth of knowledge across their chosen field. Their self-preparation for this teaching is the equivalent of another course in their curriculum, minimally guided like most advanced doctoral education, as grad students learn to become scholars. And if they're paying attention, they know their real success will come from the quality of their research. As is true of their doctoral advisors, teaching is a secondary responsibility, to be done as efficiently as possible while they scan the horizon for jobs and grants.

DIFFERENT INTENTIONS, DIFFERENT OUTCOMES

These are the four fundamental higher education ecosystems, each containing its own unique form of student-faculty interrelationships. The question of contingent faculty, the "adjunct crisis," cannot be talked about as though it were a uniform phenomenon occurring equally across all of the bioregions of higher education. The quantity and role of contingency looks sharply different at different kinds of institutions, as is shown in table 2.

Contingency affects all areas of higher education, but some kinds of schools are subjected to it more than others. As is true in so many areas of our financially stratified society, those students who need the greatest assistance get the least, while the benefits flow to those who already have them.

A lot of higher-education cheerleading—from within the academy, from legislators pushing workforce development, and from think tanks promoting degree attainment—relies upon a common statement: *People with college degrees will earn more over their careers than people without college.*

TABLE 2 Ecosystems of higher education

Type	Working-class	Middle-class	Affluent professional	Executive
Kinds of schools	Community colleges, trade schools	State comprehensive universities, lesser-known liberal arts colleges	Elite liberal arts colleges	Flagship state universities, private research universities
Student selectivity	Open to all	Moderately selective	Highly selective on grades, test scores, and creativity	Highly selective on grades, test scores, and swagger
Endowment	Minuscule; meaningless to daily operation	Millions; mostly used for financial aid	Hundreds of millions; mostly used for financial aid and for niceties of life	Billions; a crucial component of institutional operations
Tuition cost	Low to very low	Relatively low for in-state students in publics; relatively high for out-of-state students and privates	High to very high	Relatively high for in-state students in publics; high to very high for out-of-state students and privates
Transfer students	Constant	Many	Very few	Few at publics, very few at privates
Contingent faculty	Strong majority	Majority	Minority, sometimes a very small minority	Minority, mostly grad students and lecturers in gen-ed courses

As Paul Fussell might say, "But no." Any aggregation of outcomes masks a wide disparity of individual realities. A student from a well-to-do family getting her degree in public policy from Columbia University and staying in New York City is going to have different financial outcomes than a low-income student getting her degree in early childhood education from Ferris State University and staying in Big Rapids, Michigan. The national average starting wage for college grads might be fifty thousand dollars, but the specifics will vary wildly.

Higher ed leaders and policymakers talk easily and earnestly about the "college wage premium"—the notion that college provides a substantial boost to earnings immediately after college, and provides opportunities for substantial earning growth after a decade or two in one's career. But that's a misstatement of conditions on the ground. It's not that college gets you a good job; the average wage for college degree holders has been relatively flat for thirty years. Instead, it's that the *lack of college* sets you up to have a terrible job, or no job at all. College has become a form of indispensable employment insurance, available for purchase on the open market at protection levels from community college bronze to Ivy League platinum.

Students and parents, more than policy makers or college leaders, better understand the real fact of the matter: in recent decades, the number of decently-paid jobs open to high-school grads has plummeted [25] at least in part because there are so many college grads that they're forced to take jobs once occupied by high-school grads.[26] The college wage premium would more accurately be called the "college wage defense," the credential that acts as a life raft in dangerous waters. It's no surprise that everybody wants one; the alternative is life-threatening.[27]

But if everybody got to play major league baseball, the games would be a lot less fun to watch. So too, when 70 percent of all American high school grads go off to college; a great number of college classes won't be much fun to teach. Those courses—at non-selective schools, at off-hours, teaching eighth-grade reading skills or the basics of a discipline to first- and second-year students who are likely to drop out—are the ones that are remanded to the contingent community. The fun courses for carefully selected students of advanced standing . . . those are the ones that the TT faculty claim for themselves.

4

BUILDING THE
CONTINGENT WORKFORCE

Most undergraduates don't realize that there is a shrinking percentage of positions in the humanities that offer job security, benefits, and a livable salary (though it is generally much lower than salaries in other fields requiring as many years of training). They don't know that you probably will have to accept living almost anywhere, and that you must also go through a six-year probationary period at the end of which you may be fired for any number of reasons and find yourself exiled from the profession. They seem to think becoming a humanities professor is a reliable prospect—a more responsible and secure choice than, say, attempting to make it as a freelance writer, or an actor, or a professional athlete—and, as a result, they don't make any fallback plans until it is too late.

—William Pannapacker, "Graduate School in the Humanities:
      Just Don't Go."[1]

Because my husband's a doctor, he doesn't understand the academic job market. He's like, "You spend all this time preparing and there's no guaranteed job when you're done?" He believes me when I tell him, but he doesn't get it.

—Helen, doctoral student and former adjunct

Adjuncting can be pretty awful work. Low pay, no benefits, no security, no intellectual freedom. Why would anybody ever do it? Where do all of these serfs come from to work their overlords' estates?

GLUTTING THE MARKET

My wife (Ph.D. environmental psychology, CUNY Graduate Center, 1982) recently got an alumni solicitation letter from the psychology program's "acting executive officer" (a nonacademic title that says a lot about the institution's values) crowing about the status of the program and asking for dough. Along with the bragging points about $25 million in recent funding from the federal alphabet science agencies (NIH, NSF, NICHD), they had this glowing bit of news:

> Over the past 5 years (2012–2016), we produced 337 Ph.D.'s, many of whom are receiving this letter now as alumni! Congratulations, and I hope that your careers have been successfully launched.

Well, first off, "hope" is not a strategy, as the saying goes. Does the psych graduate program actually *do* anything to make sure that its doctoral alumni have successfully launched careers? Probably not so much. But the aggravating factor is just the raw numbers. This acceptably good program, ranked in the broad middling band of the nation's 185 doctoral psych programs by the National Research Council, has produced an average of nearly seventy new PhDs a year? Into a job market that accepts only a few hundred new tenure track hires nationwide? And they're *proud* of that? It's like training gladiators to be fed to the lions. As the faculty critic Marc Bousquet says, the PhD is now correctly understood as the *end* of one's academic career, and new doctoral recipients are viewed as waste products to be discarded after their utility as low-paid research and teaching staff has ended.[2]

The National Science Foundation's Survey of Earned Doctorates shows 3,765 new PhDs in psychology in 2014. These people entered a hiring pool that the *Chronicle of Higher Education*'s JobTracker research project estimated at 326 tenure-track positions at four-year schools for the 2013–14 academic year. That's one faculty job for every eleven and a half new scholars.

But grad students make cheap teachers and cheap lab assistants, keeping a forty-fourth-ranked doctoral program afloat so that its director can send out fundraising letters and its faculty can rake in research funds with all that grad-student labor. Really, it's not much different from a payday lending operation: a way for those already wealthy to scrape a few more dollars out of the pockets of the desperate, leaving them on the streets when they've run dry. It's the immigrant story, the hopes of climbers and strivers who don't recognize the secret passwords they'll need to get into the club.

In 1960, American universities graduated 9,733 new PhDs across all fields. By 1975, when the baby boomers were coming through the doctoral door, there were 32,952. In 2015, that number had grown to 55,006.[3] Fifty-five thousand people, coming into a job pool that might accept twenty thousand a year,[4] and then competing with all the people who didn't get jobs the year before. And the year before that, ad infinitum. It's an ugly job market, the boom that drives the bust.

But some people do get jobs, after all. Some people win the lottery, too, which is what keeps the rest of us in line at the mini-mart. What exactly is it that differentiates the powerful wolf from the overpopulated, starving coyotes? How does a new scholar make herself noticed among all the other wildlife?

STARTING ON THIRD BASE

The National Research Council has done a massive reputational study in doctoral education, attempting to rank all American research doctoral programs in all known fields.[5] The methodology is complex and seems reasonable, but one thing to consider before we get to the findings is just how large they've discovered the enterprise to be, with more than 4,800 different PhD-granting programs located at about 210 institutions:

- agricultural sciences (of various sorts): 317 doctoral programs
- biological sciences: 989

- health sciences: 189
- physical sciences (including math): 916
- engineering: 798
- social sciences: 930
- humanities: 866

Within this broad landscape, the findings are as you might expect: the general peer rankings of different departments within the same field are not the same. There are doctoral programs that are uniformly perceived to be disciplinary leaders, and doctoral programs that scarcely anyone knows about unless they're directly reminded of them. Just as is true for undergraduate programs, a doctoral degree from a high-end program has more resume weight than a doctorate from a lesser program. It doesn't guarantee a TT position by any means, but it makes it far more likely that an application (one of hundreds received for every job) will make it to the second round where someone will actually read it.

Doctoral reputation rankings are similar to, but not congruent with, the overall ranking of institutions. For instance, not all Ivy League colleges are premier locations for doctoral study in philosophy; for that, you'd rather go to Stanford, Michigan, or NYU than to Yale or Cornell. But in general, the research-centered programs at the elite schools are seen to be the most prestigious, and they confer that prestige upon their PhD graduates.[6] This absolutely *does not* mean that their graduates will be better teachers; in fact, since they've been trained as leading-edge researchers and rewarded for research competency, they may have spent far less time learning the classroom craft than their colleagues from lesser-ranked programs. But when hiring time comes, the reputation points still accrue to the research-focused programs.

Table 3 shows a look at a few example disciplines, with the top ten doctoral programs for each.[7] A quick glance at the list shows the names you'd expect: Yale, NYU, Harvard, Michigan, Stanford, Chicago, Duke.[8] But the specifics of individual disciplines reveal a few schools that you'd never imagine as top-ten candidates, but which

TABLE 3 The top of the top, by discipline

Discipline	Top ten doctoral programs
American studies	Yale, NYU, SUNY Buffalo, Indiana, Minnesota, William and Mary, Maryland, Michigan State, New Mexico, Kansas
Anthropology	Harvard, Penn State, Michigan, Arizona, Berkeley, Duke, UCLA, UC-Irvine, Chicago, Emory
Biochemistry	Stanford, Wisconsin, Brandeis, Washington, Wash U (St. Louis), Duke, Vanderbilt, Rutgers, SUNY Rochester, Case Western Reserve
Chemical engineering	Caltech, Texas, Berkeley, MIT, UC-Santa Barbara, Minnesota, Princeton, Michigan, Stanford, Wisconsin
Economics	Harvard, MIT, Chicago, Princeton, Berkeley, NYU, Stanford, Penn, Yale, Northwestern
History	Princeton, Harvard, Chicago, Johns Hopkins, Columbia, Stanford, NYU, Penn, Berkeley, North Carolina
Linguistics	Penn, Chicago, Maryland, Stanford, Berkeley, Massachusetts, Northwestern, Ohio State, MIT, USC
Mathematics	Princeton, NYU, Berkeley, Stanford, Harvard, Michigan, MIT, Penn State, Wisconsin, Caltech
Philosophy	Chicago, Princeton, Rutgers, Michigan, Berkeley, NYU, MIT, Stanford, Carnegie Mellon, Pittsburgh
Sociology	Princeton, Harvard, Penn, Michigan, Columbia, Texas, North Carolina, Duke, Stanford, Chicago
Zoology	Wisconsin, Washington, Oregon State, Miami, Washington State, Michigan State, North Carolina State, Hawaii, Florida, Oklahoma

Source: National Research Council, "Data-Based Assessment of Research-Doctorate Programs"

are powerhouses in their particular field of knowledge: Buffalo, William and Mary, and New Mexico for American studies, Brandeis for biochem, Oregon State and Hawaii for zoology. Outsiders (including most college students considering grad school) have no reason to know this; insiders do.

As the oversupply of doctorate holders increases, it's not merely that those with degrees from lesser schools will get teaching jobs at lesser schools, because those schools too are now receiving faculty applications from graduates of the uppermost programs, who can't all teach at top-tier schools themselves. So schools all the way down to the state comprehensives are also selecting faculty who graduated from the elite programs, not from the merely excellent. One young assistant professor I know, recently hired into a decidedly non-elite undergraduate biology program, has a PhD from a top-5-percent doctoral program and served a multiyear postdoc with one of the agencies of the National Institutes of Health. That's a powerful mismatch between training and employment; and, given that she chose to go to an elite school and an elite lab, it seems as though teaching introductory courses in ecology and evolution might bore her before long. So her new school has to spend money on research infrastructure to keep her interested and professionally productive, drawing the school away from its core undergraduate education mission. (In another decade, she'll probably have a doctoral program of her own).

What of the lower-level doctoral programs? Here are a few examples. Let's leave them unnamed:

- a public university with none of its eleven PhD programs ranked in the top half of their respective disciplines; seven of the eleven were in the lowest quartile of their fields
- a public university with none of its seventeen doctoral programs in the top half of their fields, and with thirteen of those seventeen in the bottom quartile
- a private university with only one of its fourteen doctoral programs in the top half of its field, barely, and eleven of the fourteen in the bottom quartile.

What exactly are those schools selling, and to whom? What exactly do their students believe they are buying?

Those doctoral programs exist because of the benefits they confer upon their institutions and their TT faculty, far more than because of their benefits to grad-student consumers. Doctoral programs allow universities better chances to attract research funding, to have the prestige of seeing their Carnegie Classification move from master's to doctoral institution, to let their faculty argue for smaller teaching loads in light of greater graduate-advising responsibilities, and to provide an army of teaching and research staff who'll work for nothing more than a tuition waiver.

Most schools have no vested interest in telling prospective students any of this, if they want them to enroll. But it's crucial to understand that the simple existence of a doctoral program does not mean that the doctorates issued thereby will be recognized as equal currency. Any doctoral degree will be read by faculty search committees in three components: "I have a PhD in [discipline] from [university and department], studying under [dissertation advisor]." An individual's faculty job chances are dependent on each of those terms, far more than the fact of their graduate GPA.[9]

STERILE HYBRIDS

Another flaw in doctoral production is the increase in the numbers of interdisciplinary PhD-producing programs that have no analogue in the PhD-consuming disciplinary marketplace. As scholars become more senior, they often find their intellectual interests expanding beyond the boundaries of a single discipline. This has resulted in hybrid programs: crosses of social science with architecture (such as my own field of environment-behavior studies), history with engineering (history of science and technology), world languages with anthropology and political science (Asian studies, for instance), and so on. When funding or persuasiveness has allowed, they've become programs with their own graduate students. They're fascinating programs, and they contribute to important new ways of understanding the phenomena around us. But as fun as the mating may have been for the parents, most of their mongrel offspring will ultimately be sterile. The horse parents have their safe home in the horse pasture, and the donkey parents have their safe home in the donkey barn, but their graduate-student mule is born to do lots and lots of really

useful work, and then to never be accepted within any fertile partner community. As long as the hiring in higher education is done
by departments, this will never, ever change. The mongrels will be
shunned as being not really part of any originating herd, and unable
to develop a viable new species. But they'll be useful for dragging the
scholarly cart, advancing the intellectual cause for a few more miles
before being left dead at the side of the road.[10]

Interdisciplinarity is a privilege reserved for those already established within the walls of academic life. In 2014, the Eighth Annual
Global Summit on Graduate Education developed a statement of
support of interdisciplinary graduate education, even recommend-
ing that universities "value interdisciplinary mentoring or research in
faculty tenure and promotion procedures." This series of principles,
however, was silent about hiring practices, leaving the incoming
scholar to fend for herself.[11] As one commentator put it, "Interdisciplinarity can be a red flag. It signals to the administration that you
don't necessarily fit in our department, and department identity is
crucial in these times of tight budgets. We really want you to learn
to be interdisciplinary after we hire you, not before."[12]

In the face of doctoral overpopulation, there's been talk about
restricting the numbers of people who get PhDs each year, mostly
framed in terms of reducing the numbers of entrants (again putting
the burden onto the individual student or prospective student). Why
don't we talk in terms of putting the burden onto the institution?
Why should we have 4,800 departmental issuers of the PhD, when
we know that only a fraction of those will offer productive gate-
ways to faculty life?[13] Why should those 4,800 programs have tens
of thousands of faculty who can lead dissertations, only a fraction of
whom are willing or capable of offering strong mentorship into academic life? Why shouldn't we make each department and each dissertation advisor demonstrate their graduates' outcomes every few
years, letting the unproductive and the hybrids fall away?

LASER-FOCUSED FROM BIRTH:
AGE DISCRIMINATION BEGINS AT THIRTY

A lot of senior college faculty came up in an era of doctoral under-production, when both the number and the scope of colleges were growing faster than the supply of qualified faculty. They kept their jobs and moved forward even as the next generation found the barriers to entry increasing. This has been true in a great number of professions, by the way; a recent study by the Federal Reserve Bank of St. Louis found that during the past fifteen years, older workers who already had jobs remained employed in significant numbers, but younger workers entering the market had a much harder time getting through the door.[14] For higher education, with its aging faculty set never to retire, the barriers are even greater.

> "It was not only naîveté, but perhaps also a sensibility shared with my cohort that came of age intellectually at the end of the 1960s that led me to make the choice of profession without much soul searching. . . ."
> —John Komlos[15]

That haphazard approach to faculty career development may have been viable at the end of the 1960s—and a little further on, we'll discuss the baby boomer wave that made it possible. But now that the ecosystem is overpopulated, becoming a college faculty member isn't much different from becoming an elite athlete: it takes intellectual and logistical focus from earliest childhood. Anyone pursuing the path in as casual a fashion as Komlos implies is likely to crash as quickly and spectacularly as a taxi driver in the Indianapolis 500.

Oh, and Komlos conveniently neglects to mention that his master's and PhD in history were from the University of Chicago, then as now a top-five research school in that discipline, and that he was mentored by Nobel-winning economist Robert Fogel. Nah, he just sort of stumbled into it all.

Many of my interviews with adjunct faculty showed them to be relative latecomers to their fields (as was I):

I did my undergrad in international relations, thinking I'd follow my father into government work. I decided I didn't want that, did a master's in English, then a doctoral program.

My [master's] advisor pushed me to become an academic. "You're good with students, you've been published, you're really good at this. . . ." I sort of fell into it.

I'd always wanted to be a teacher. I had teaching experience in high school, college, and grad school; it was just a part of my identity. I didn't want to be a professor, I didn't know what that was about, didn't know that role. But my undergraduate advisor said, Did you ever consider being a professor? It's so funny to think about it, how that one conversation over coffee changed my career. I knew that I loved thinking about ideas, loved having conversations about these issues, but the idea of being a professor was just alien.

My parents were both doctors. My father has a doctorate in statistics. My mother was a medical doctor, a physician. They think I should have gone into finance and gotten a job in a bank. I did an MBA in finance, and then the PhD in art history.

I was always into art but it wasn't really encouraged in my house, so I went ahead and did the poli-sci thing, hoping to join the foreign service. They had a hiring freeze on from my undergrad all through grad school, so I decided to take a big life jump and do what I loved—art and architecture.

Becoming a TT faculty member now is no different from becoming a professional hockey player. You start at four or five, you move up through the developmental leagues, you play for the national junior team, maybe go to college at an NCAA Frozen Four school. (As Malcolm Gladwell notes in his book *Outliers*, it'll also help to have been born just after the age-group cutoff dates, and thus to have always been the biggest, strongest kid at every age level along the way.) Your competitors will have had every advantage life can offer, and you have to match them somehow.

In academic life, that means moving directly from a home with books and ideas through a strong undergraduate program and into a strong doctoral program, with no significant time away for work or musing on one's life.[16] It means moving swiftly through that doctoral program, preferably working in research assistantships that foster both coauthorship and recognition by major funding agencies, rather than teaching assistantships that mark one as a member of the anonymous service class. Arriving at the doctorate by one's late twenties or early thirties, the new scholar is then recognizable by similarly trained and similarly privileged colleagues. The historian L. Maren Wood has compiled data in the humanities that show more than 50 percent of new tenure-track hires were either in the very final stages of completing their dissertations or not more than a year post-PhD, with the number of hires for those each year past graduation tailing away to invisibility.[17] In the physical sciences, a laboratory postdoc can act as a sort of date renewal after grad school, but in any case, the clock begins to tick more loudly at the end of one's most current research apprenticeship.

I recently returned from the Bread Loaf Writer's Conference. My workshop leader, the wonderful novelist Peter Ho Davies (a faculty member at Michigan), had marked up the opening chapters of a novel I'm working on. The character mentions that he's got a PhD and recently finished a postdoc; he's thirty-one, and I thought that was a pretty accurate status to expect, perhaps even a bit aggressive. Peter circled both of those points, and wrote in the margin, "Making him 27 or 28?" Peter himself became a TT faculty member at thirty. I finished my own PhD at thirty-eight, and finished my first postdoc at forty-eight, my bar code clearly marking me as an expired package destined for the dollar store.[18]

YOU CAN'T JOIN THE LODGE WITHOUT A SPONSOR

The business writer Harvey Coleman developed a recipe for career success based on performance, image, and exposure (or, because business gurus can't go two sentences without an acronym, PIE).[19] Coleman further does some faux quantification to assert that career success is 10 percent performance, 30 percent image, and 60 percent exposure. While I don't buy the precision of those numbers, I think that the general impulse is correct. Our myth of meritocracy has us believe that performance is everything, whereas it's merely a threshold measurement that then allows the other two components to come into play. Poor performance absolutely keeps a scholar from moving forward, but high performance merely gets her into the second round, to be reviewed on the two criteria that matter more.

Performance will be measured in proxy by a job candidate's doctoral degree program, her record of publication and presentation, and her ability to help in obtaining research funding. These areas of performance are largely under the individual job candidate's control, but not entirely. For instance, if a doctoral student isn't in a highly equipped lab or surrounded by the institutional resources necessary for getting grants in her specialty, her grant record just won't be as good as if she'd been at a top-tier school. If her library isn't as well staffed as the remarkable Doe Library at Berkeley, she won't get the same one-on-one bibliographic assistance or advice about key journals and archives. So, as brilliant as an individual grad student may be, she needs the tools to deploy that brilliance — tools not uniformly available at all universities or from all advisors.

The *image* part of the formula is in large part genetic, though a good tailor and time spent at the gym will help. But part of one's image has to do with how a hiring committee will read candidates — a reading entirely out of a candidate's control. For instance, someone in their forties will have a terrible time in a competitive job market, because the image of a new faculty colleague is a person in her early thirties. A woman of childbearing age wearing a wedding ring will be seen as a hazard, because her imagined productivity is likely to be damaged by her imagined motherhood. A person of color will have a harder time passing the "good fit for our department" threshold in a department that's always been all white. We've long known that these unspoken but real markers set people up for success or exclusion just as much as the variable of performance.[20]

The *exposure* component, the largest, is the responsibility of the new scholar's dissertation committee members far more than it is of the doctoral student herself. No community welcomes new members without a sponsor, a current member willing to do the work of introducing, lending support, making connections, and easing the way. Again, we have the common failure of imagination that supposes that everything we need to know about education happens in a classroom. But the real work of making a doctoral student into a viable colleague is done by the faculty, outside of class time.

One of my own doctoral program's former faculty had a monthly dinner at her home for all of her dissertation students, in which they reviewed one another's CVs and cover letters. She worked with her students to help them locate openings and cast their research into the best possible language for that specific program. Among her colleagues in the profession, she got her students behind some doors that otherwise would have been closed to them, making introductions and building alliances with senior scholars in a position to hire. And sure enough, her students did far better on the job market than those of any of her colleagues. The work of mentorship is knowable, and must be approached with the same rigor as any other part of intellectual life for one's doctoral students to become faculty themselves.

Doctoral programs in the United States are divided into two periods: coursework, concluded by comprehensive exams and a proposal for a dissertation, and then dissertator status, in which the fully vetted student works on her own research. A doctoral faculty member and doctoral program that do not work steadily for the entirety of each student's dissertator period to help them gain entry to the academic profession have committed malpractice. They are complicit in selling intelligent, proven students an expensive property and then letting them be foreclosed upon. As is always true in bubble economies, the salespeople try to wash their hands of it; but that stain will not be removed.

CULTURAL MISFITS IN THE ALT-CAREER MARKET

There's a lot of commentary in doctoral education circles about preparing students for "alt-careers," bringing their intelligence to bear in a variety of industries rather than focusing only upon an academic livelihood. Although all those adjuncts and postdocs could leave, could go on into lives in pharma or finance (and make more money than they would as professors anyway), most careers are misfit for the mindset engendered by a good doctoral education. Jean-Paul Sartre once described the intellectual classes as "organic intellectuals," those organically grown by commerce to serve its own needs, and "critical intellectuals," those who ask larger questions and concern themselves with issues beyond the technical and functional: issues of justice, ethics, and uncertainty.[21]

Commerce rewards expertise, that thing that you know you can do reliably and quickly. Academic life rewards almost the inverse condition, a constant state of "not-knowing," a discontent with current knowledge and current practice, a desire to reexamine the foundations of one's knowledge. There's a reason why the academic doctorate is called *Doctor of Philosophy*; regardless of the discipline, the PhD is training to be critical, to live within what Martha Graham once called "a queer, divine dissatisfaction, a blessed unrest." This is a dissatisfaction not sated within a bank or brokerage, not responsive to quarterly investment summaries, not fueled by the work of managing a supermarket or a state office. In my experience, it's equally ill fed by the work of academic administration, which has closer familial relations to running a restaurant than to being a scholar.

The work of the doctorate, done well, makes its participants ill shaped for other ways of living. They cling to academic career hopes in the face of evidence—not merely out of wishful thinking that someday they might be allowed inside the academic gates, but because it's the way scholars understand the world, and because other careers are less open to curiosity.

BAIT AND SWITCH

I told them I wanted a full-time position, and they told me there was no money to create that, so I quit in summer 2016, after ten years. Then they got the money to create the tenure-track position, and I've applied.
— Niccole, adjunct faculty

When I took the [adjunct] job at [my college], I totally had the foot-in-the-door mindset. I was a finalist for a full-time non-TT position they created, and I could really feel the disadvantage of being a parent of small children. Also, I discovered by accident that one of my colleagues was also a finalist, and she'd been with the school for twenty-five years. As it turns out, neither one of us got it.
— Rebecca, adjunct faculty

The landscape of being allowed in changed. Positions disappeared during the hiring process, or became fake — they'd hire someone off the page, not connected to their job description. Positions that were intended as permanent became one-year with possible renewal. They'd be advertised as tenure-track, but mysteriously become year-to-year during the process.
— Paul, adjunct faculty

We can focus on flaws in production as a part of contingency, but we can't let go of the problem without also focusing on flaws in consumption.

In my conversations with contingent faculty, one of the things I heard often was a sense of having been baited. Some school opened up a few courses and implied (in some vague and therefore legally defensible way) that they constituted a "position," and that success at those courses could lead to a permanent faculty line "soon." So the happy, excited teacher had a great semester or a great year, and the department chair told her what a great job she was doing and how happy they were to have her. She got those two courses again, plus maybe a third one. At any other job, this would be a clear sign that she was being groomed for promotion.

And so the trap is baited, so the trap is sprung.

Adjunct positions do not morph into tenure-track positions, and adjunct workers are not offered permanence on the basis of their good work. Tenure-track job openings—even at a fifth-tier school, a Northwestern Central A&M State Tech—are the subjects of national searches. Colleges don't hire people on spec to try them out. Teachers don't work their way up. A postdoc or an adjunct teaching position is exactly and only that, an offer to do specific work for a specific time for a specific dollar amount, with no guarantee of further relations. The contingent worker is not only not guaranteed the job if it ever materializes, but is likely diminishing her chances by (a) accumulating more time since her dissertation and thereby going stale, and (b) being seen as "just a teacher" and thus a diminished scholar. I have a friend who was a highly regarded adjunct at a major Eastern research university for three years. She was so highly regarded, in fact, that they asked her to serve on the search committee for the tenure-track line that her chair told her not to bother applying for—because she was, after all, just a teacher.

But the bait is so, so appealing. It's fun to be back in the classroom. It's gratifying to have an e-mail address ending in .edu. It's heady to have the chair tell you how highly she thinks of your work, and to read the students' pleasure (in you and in their own capabilities) in your course evaluations. Magical thinking takes over, and adjuncts can invest years in a half-promised permanence that they believe they might somehow earn.

It is morally indefensible to lure people to teach at an institution in the vague hope that they might someday become a permanent faculty member. I understand that circumstances change without warning, that a budgeted TT line might not materialize in the face of actual enrollment declines. But it happens far too often, to far too many intelligent people, for one to imagine that it's accidental every time. Colleges have benefitted from the lack of clarity about both the short-term and the long-term implications of their contracts, leaving their contingent suitors perpetually uncertain. Is there any meaningful hope of a faithful, permanent relationship, or should they just be satisfied with the envelope on the nightstand?

5

IF WE DON'T PAY TEACHERS, WHY IS MY TUITION SO HIGH?

We all know the stories of skyrocketing tuition, and parallel increases in student loan debt. American college graduates (and those who tried college but didn't graduate) collectively owe about $1.4 trillion in student loans — more than all in American car loans, more than all of American credit-card debt, and second only to our mortgages. Tuition has risen about three times faster than inflation since I started college in 1976. Table 4 shows the changes to national average tuition, all inflation-adjusted to match 2017 dollars.[1]

On its face, this just makes no sense. During the period in which colleges doubled their reliance on low-paid contingent faculty, they also tripled their prices? Man, somebody must be getting rich!

Well, yes, but not necessarily who you'd expect. Higher ed costs are rising steeply even with adjunct teachers, just as medical costs are rising steeply even with the shift toward paraprofessional medical staff, and for many of the same reasons. Let's explore some of the underlying reasons why increased income hasn't supported a large, stable faculty.

WHERE DO COLLEGES GET MONEY?

Colleges and universities, regardless of size or complexity, essentially have some mixture of the same three income sources: pay-

TABLE 4   Tuition increases, 1976–77 to 2016–17, adjusted for inflation

	In-state tuition		
	Public two-year colleges	Public four-year colleges	Private four-year colleges
1976–77	$1,210	$2,650	$10,860
1986–87	$1,480	$3,160	$14,880
1996–97	$2,280	$4,640	$20,260
2006–7	$2,730	$6,980	$26,830
2016–17	$3,530	$9,840	$34,100
Forty-year comparison	292%	371%	314%

Source: College Board, "Tuition and Fees"

ment for services, contributions from state taxes or religious sponsors, and income from investments and gifts.

For most of American higher ed history, those three nutrient streams had predictable effects. The first, payment for services, took the form of tuition paid by parents, and the return for that payment was an assurance that their sons (and later, daughters) would be "properly finished." The second stream, sponsorship, fostered responsiveness to the social and philosophical goals of the larger agencies. And the third, gifts and the resulting endowment, allowed independence: a pool of screw-you money that opened a little breathing room from consumer and sponsor demands and blips in financial affairs.

Those three components still exist, but each has become far more complex. The payment for services still includes tuition and housing, of course, but colleges have become far more savvy at monetizing their other assets. In small ways, they make money from renting out parts of campus in the summer for soccer camps, adult-education weeks, and academic conferences. They provide consulting services for the local business community, advising on research design, marketing plans, and agricultural practices. They offer continuing education courses and seminars. They sell licensing for innumerable consumer products: logo sweatshirts and mascot mugs and college-seal smartphone covers, ice coolers for tailgating, and bar stools for your man cave.

For bigger state universities and private research schools, grants for funded research have become a crucial component of the income stream. American universities receive tens of billions of dollars in federal research funds, and billions more from research partnerships with the biomedical and pharmaceutical and agricultural industries. To take an extreme example, MIT made $340 million on tuition in 2015–16, barely a fifth of the almost $1.7 billion it made from research funding.[2] There's also a deferred payment pool that comes along with the research, as universities' inventions become patents, which in turn become licensing fees. These are not really colleges anymore; these are national laboratories that happen to have schools attached.

Even at a far less research-focused regional school like Western Michigan University, research grants and contracts amounted to 7 percent of the school's income stream for the year.[3] The importance of research money has radically shifted the attentions of larger universities. Smaller universities have followed suit, each hoping to drill its own well into the research reservoir.

The second pool of funding, sponsorship from religious denominations or state governments, has diminished radically in recent years. Private schools have often broken formal ties with their denominational founders, and organized religions aren't as flush as they were fifty years ago anyway. For public institutions, state appropriations for higher education have not kept pace with increased costs over the recent decades. The American Institutes for Research has found that just in the ten years between 2003 and 2013, public funding per student has decreased by 9 percent at community colleges, 16 percent at baccalaureate schools, 25 percent at master's schools, and 28 percent at doctoral/research universities.[4] Slowly climbing tax dollars have not matched highly increasing enrollments, nor have they matched the greater array of academic and student support services that colleges now provide. Here in Vermont, a little more than half of the state college system's funding came from its state appropriation in 1980; that's now down to about 19 percent.[5] In my home state of Michigan, public funding has done the same, from about 60 percent of state college revenues in the mid 1980s to about 20 percent now.[6]

Some of that has to do with partisan politics and the "red shift" of state legislatures. Education researcher Christopher Newfield has carefully documented the relatively recent history of manufactured public suspicion about intellectual life, in a continuous line from the efforts of the House Un-American Activities Commission to William Powell and the US Chamber of Commerce to the contemporary "liberal bias" mythmakers, all of it serving to reduce Americans' trust in and support for the broader functions of the college experience.[7] And it's worked, with Americans now showing a strong partisan divide in attitudes toward higher education: 58 percent of Republican respondents to a 2017 Pew Research Center poll believed that colleges and universities "have a negative effect on the way things are going in the country," while 72 percent of Democratic respondents believed that colleges and universities are a positive force in our nation.[8] This is not a good position from which state legislatures can develop bipartisan funding plans.

Another, less partisan explanation comes from the fact that state legislatures fund their higher education systems because of perceived regional economic benefits. But the returns on college support are less localized than they once were, and thus are less attractive to local spending. One of the reasons that rural places have been hostile to the "educated elites" is that education is almost exclusively a one-way door from country to city. Why would agricultural, mining, or timbering communities have any interest in losing even more of their smartest and most capable children? As more schools recruit out-of-state students, and more of their highly successful grads go off to metropolitan centers in other regions, state governments find higher education a less attractive funding target.

Then there's the third income stream: gifts and investments. Trust me, the local community college isn't getting much by way of alumni donation, whereas Ivy League presidents are hired on the basis of

their ability to marshal multi-billion-dollar philanthropic campaigns. Remember MIT and its annual $340 million tuition reve-
nue? In that same year, it received $162 million in operating gifts and
bequests, and the annual 5 percent payout from its $14.8 billion en-
dowment netted $731 million in operating funds, more than double
its tuition income.[9] Put another way, that single year's distribution
from MIT's endowment could pay every cent of the operation of
nearby Bunker Hill Community College and its thirteen thousand
students. For eight years.[10]

INCOME INSTABILITY, WORKER INSTABILITY

One of the unspoken assets of an elite college, whether a liberal arts
school like Reed College or a state flagship like the University of Oregon, is a brand so desirable that more students will choose it than it
can accommodate. Selectivity is a wonderful tool for income management, because it allows a college to predict with fair precision
how much money it will have on hand come fall. Other schools are
left to guess every year, and that's a strong force toward contingency.

Let's imagine a humble college. Call it, for the moment, Harvard. Harvard is shooting every year for an optimally sized freshman class, a cohort it is prepared to serve at its expected level of
care: about 1,650 to 1,700 students. For its entering class of fall 2017,
Harvard attracted almost 40,000 applicants for those 1,700 seats,
and it accepted 2,038.[11] About 17 percent of those who were accepted
went elsewhere, leaving the college right on target without having
to scrape any crumbs out of the waiting list. Harvard has the perfect tools for managing enrollment, which are high demand and
high selectivity. It can award acceptance to a couple of thousand
students every year—whether the applicant pool is thirty thousand,
sixty thousand, or two hundred thousand—and hit its budget almost
exactly.

Let's now imagine an even more humble college. Call it SOTH
(Something Other Than Harvard) State University. SOTH State is
also looking for an optimally sized freshman class to fill its classrooms

and dormitory beds, maybe a similar size of 1,650 students. But because it has a largely regional draw, and because the high achievers within that region have all applied to Harvard, SOTH State only gets three thousand applications, 10 percent or less of the applicant pool of the elite schools. It accepts 75 percent of all applicants—not the 5 percent of Harvard—to get a qualified pool of about 2,300, and then its administrators hope like hell that three-quarters of *those* applicants choose SOTH State and not some fancier address. For reasons entirely out of its control, SOTH State has to be prepared to see a freshman class of anywhere between 1,500 and 1,800, and to staff those classrooms accordingly.

The Massachusetts state universities, for example, have seen their overall enrollment go from 167,000 in 1988 to below 150,000 in 1996, back up to nearly 200,000 in 2012, and back down to 186,000 in 2016.[12] Over that same time period, schools of an even larger system, the California Community Colleges, have ranged back and forth between two and three million students per year, shifting up and down by as many as a quarter of a million from one year to the next.[13]

These are not trends that lend themselves to stable faculty employment.

The ubiquity of college leads the entire enterprise to be more susceptible to the vagaries of baby booms and busts. Lots of colleges felt this acutely in the post-2010 crash of high school graduates, with schools across the country struggling to make their enrollment targets in the face of the blunt fact of fewer 1990s babies headed to college in the 2010s. Working-class and middle-class schools have struggled with enrollment for nearly a decade, not because they're mismanaged but because there just aren't enough children.

This perfectly predictable enrollment trough somehow seemed to catch a lot of schools by surprise. They spent the 2000s ramping up their services and housing capacity and science buildings to accommodate the growth of college-aged students born in the 1980s when the hippies became yuppies, and they have spent the 2010s worrying about how to pay for all of those investments in light of enrollment collapse.

All businesses have fixed costs and unit costs, and colleges are no different. They have the fixed costs of their permanent faculty, their administration, their professional staff, their physical and informational infrastructure — costs that don't change much with shifts in demand. The unit costs are basically food and teaching, and the brunt of the unpredictability is borne by teachers who may not know until the week before the semester whether or not they'll have a particular course. For the Fall 2017 entering class, only 34 percent of surveyed colleges responded that they had completed recruitment by May 1. This means that two-thirds of schools were scrambling, many unsuccessfully, to fill their classrooms through the summer, leaving the adjunct community to wonder until the semester's start whether their sections would run.[14]

It's easy to think about this population fluidity at individual schools, but we have to understand it in the face of the collective as well. When a small fraction of high school graduates went to a small number of colleges, it was easier to calibrate for changes in population by slightly opening and closing the selectivity gates. When the substantial majority of high school graduates go to college, when the nation demands college as a necessity for adult life, the system is forced to address raw, cyclical demographics. Adjuncts are the shock absorbers that make the terrain passable.

NOMADIC STUDENTS, NOMADIC FACULTY

The stable myth of college includes the nervous freshman who arrives at Whussupwich U with the rented truck in late August after high school, and leaves exactly eight semesters later as a confident, berobed twenty-one-year-old, WU diploma in hand. This was never true for every student, but now it's a relative rarity. More than half of all students stop and start (as I did), or just stop, their progress disrupted by individual lack of interest or by family need, by sick children or a semester of work to pay for the next semester of school. Related to that, nearly 40 percent of all college graduates who started school in 2008 received their degrees from a college other than the one at which they began.[15]

This remarkable student mobility has created a massive infrastructure to support transfer credits, the ability to apply courses taken at school A to a degree later obtained at school B. The basic logic of transfer credits is functional equivalency: that is, the understanding that Calculus 1 at my school is more or less the same as Calculus 1 at your school, that "three credits of Calculus 1" is the name of a currency that a student can exchange at any institution.

This presumed equivalency leads toward what economists call commodity pricing. A simple commodity is a product that has no differentiation by producer and no intention of a relationship between producer and consumer. A hundred pounds of milk, for instance, a standard unit of measurement in the industry. It's picked up at the dairy, and pumped into the giant truck of other raw milk from everybody else. It goes through the same processes and packaging as the milk from hundreds of other dairies, and winds up in a plastic jug or a shrink-wrapped cheese in the supermarket, its molecules intermingled with those in the milk from every other farm. Every dairy farmer gets the same price per unit, with no claim to unique quality being made, except for a minimum threshold of noncontamination. It can't be any worse than the standard, but it doesn't need to be any better.

A college credit is similarly commodified. As students are mobile, as transfers are common, the three credits accumulated in Intro Sociology at one school need to be recognized and converted into three credits of Intro Sociology at another school. The uniqueness of the experience, the specific insights gained, are no longer relevant; the instructor has been eliminated from view in favor of the three credits of content she has provided, and the student likewise has been eliminated from view in favor of a person who owns three credits of content. (The very term "content" makes it clear that the unit of measurement describes volume rather than quality.) Intro

Sociology and milk are uniform and impersonal products, drawn as needed from their respective common tanks. They are fungible: non-differentiated and mutually exchangeable.[16]

The fungibility of the commodity places downward pressure on price, and cannot consider the unique practices of the producer. If a particular dairy farmer thinks he needs $18.50 per hundredweight to break even, but the going market rate from the co-op is $16.50, then $16.50 it's going to be, and the individual farmer gets to choose to (a) lose two bucks per hundred pounds, (b) reduce the quality costs of his work, or (c) stop selling milk altogether. So too for adjunct faculty. Intro Sociology can be bought by colleges in the Boston Metro teaching market for about three thousand dollars per three credits,[17] so an individual teacher—no matter how well credentialed, no matter how excellent—gets to choose to (a) teach for an embarrassingly small hourly rate, (b) try to make their teaching something simpler and less time-intensive, or (c) not teach at all. In the eyes of the college-as-aggregator, as long as any specific provider is above the floor of competency, it doesn't really matter if they're any better.

As the college *experience* is abandoned in favor of the college *credit*, it makes perfect sense to move to a Darwinian competition between desperate providers. We've made it clear, without ever naming it as a policy or a purpose, that higher education—especially for the working-class and middle-class colleges for which transfer is ubiquitous—has largely accepted the loss of the unique experience, and is willing to settle for the quantifiable product.[18] A college course should be a unique thing to be done, not a uniform product to be purchased. But the logic of exchange consumes all other ways of thinking if we aren't wary.

A school's reliance on transfer credits—both inbound and outbound—is closely related to its reliance on adjuncts. Community colleges, for instance, are almost fully in the transfer business, preparing their students to take those first two years and bolt them onto the front end of someone else's degree program. Community colleges also have the greatest collective reliance on adjunct faculty: nationally at about 70 percent, with some schools at or above 90 percent. Most middle-class colleges also have high rates of transfer flux, and those are also significant locations of adjunct instruction.

Regardless of school, it's primarily the courses that serve the majors and their departments that are taught by TT faculty. Adjunct faculty are concentrated in courses that live outside departmental majors, in the core curriculum that forms the basis of most transfers. Writing instruction is highly reliant on contingent faculty, as are lower-division math courses, science-for-nonmajors "breadth courses," and introductory social science and humanities courses. These are the courses that are treated as commodities, one product being the same as any other, produced and consumed in every landscape, teachable by faculty with less specialization and expertise. The departments often disparagingly refer to them as "service courses"—courses that fulfill larger institutional needs rather than being explicitly for students within their majors, and which thus don't deserve precious departmental resources.

The introductory service courses that make up the majority of transferrable credit also have the greatest number of nonaffiliated people who are competent enough to teach them. In any given area, there are dozens or hundreds of people who could step up to teach Mathematics for the Liberal Arts or Business Analysis; likely nobody who could take on Discrete Mathematics or Affine Geometry. The relative ease of finding adjuncts for lower-level courses keeps the permanent faculty out of them, and drives the stipends down.

Community colleges and state systems as a whole often develop elaborate articulation agreements, predetermined equivalencies that lay out which credits for which courses can be moved from one school to another. Multistate articulation agreements are increasingly developed as well, in less populous regions of the country. These articulation agreements are vital for students, who aren't forced to purchase as many redundant or make-up courses at their new schools;[19] they're brutal for the teaching profession, making contingent faculty into the equivalent of commodity farmers, a bushel of winter wheat from Montana being identical to a bushel of winter wheat from Oklahoma.

Even at the major research universities, those same lower-division courses will likely be taught by contingent faculty, whether adjuncts, graduate student teaching assistants, or postdocs. It's the flagship products, the upper-division courses where faculty interests and their specializations come into view (and which are the most fun to teach, filled with strong, committed students who have proven their earlier capability), that are invulnerable to contingency.

At the most high-end liberal arts colleges, adjuncts are scarce, in part because transfer is scarce. These schools stake their reputations on offering the irreplaceably unique experience. An elite school like Middlebury College lists 95 percent of its undergrads as "first-time, full-time" students (a mere 19 of the 2,500 students having transferred in, and almost everyone taking a full load of courses); and it graduates 93 percent of its incoming freshmen.[20] This unique experience is expensive. Middlebury has a list cost of attendance (including room and board and standard expenses) of about $69,000.[21] Students who choose an affluent professional school most often have substantial family resources to draw upon—not merely financial, but also intellectual and emotional—to weather the storms that might cause other students at other schools to delay or move their college completion.

A middle-class school like Central Michigan University is much more transfer-oriented. Only 68 percent of its students meet the federal definition of "first-time, full-time," the others either being part-time or having transferred from other schools. Of those students who started at CMU as freshmen, only 57 percent graduated from CMU in six years.[22] That doesn't mean that the other 43 percent didn't graduate from college at all; for many, it means that they finished at another school, carrying their credits along with them.

The contingent faculty watch the weather, hoping that the next growing season looks promising, and wondering whether it's time to move along themselves.

COLLEGES CHASING THE JOB MARKET

Practical education as an element of the college ecology has been around for at least as long as the Morrill Act of 1862, for "the endowment, support, and maintenance of at least one college [in each state] where the leading object shall be, without excluding other scientific and classical studies and including military tactics, to teach such branches of learning as are related to agriculture and the mechanic arts, in such manner as the legislatures of the States may respectively prescribe, in order to promote the liberal and practical education of the industrial classes in the several pursuits and professions in life."[23] (The term "agriculture and mechanic arts" is why some of these schools still have "A&M" in their names.) The Morrill grants launched many of the middle-class colleges, as did the 1890s institution of colleges specifically aimed at the needs of African-American students in states where the Morrill land-grant colleges chose to continue segregation. The nineteenth century also saw another version of vocational colleges, as normal schools emerged with their mission of making high school graduates into K–12 teachers, and small denominational colleges were founded for the production of ministers and lay leaders.

Most of these humble schools have now become middle-class state universities like the University of Wisconsin–Milwaukee or Kent State University, and a few are elite, major universities like UCLA, Michigan State, and even MIT. These were — and, except for the elite handful, still are — places where the children of farmers and mechanics could absorb white-collar norms. Those students were not merely learning trades like teaching, pastoring, or engineering; more important, they were learning to behave and believe as middle-class people did. Regardless of major, these colleges were where young people learned temperance and diligence and cooperation, and where they learned to take their places within the management of increasingly complex industrial and civic and social systems. They were the launching grounds of the industrial revolution. Let the Ivies remain for the sons of princes to learn finance and strategy, the nation said; the great bursting forth of nineteenth-century colleges was America making its robust future, staking its profit on innovation and industry.

American higher education, in its working-class and middle-class forms, is still largely vocational, aimed at a generational quality-of-life shift from worker to manager, from outdoor to indoor labor, from dangerous to safe jobs, from getting by to getting ahead. But at least two things have changed since the Morrill Act. One is that, since the heyday of the New Deal and the Great Society, the goals of collective good and planned economy have increasingly been supplanted by belief in the invisible hand of individual tactical decisions. No Congress today would put forth a lasting national plan like the Morrill Act, much less the Works Progress Administration or Social Security or the Higher Education Act of 1965; we have been converted to the presumed wisdom of the market, the tide of individuals' choices somehow representing moral direction rather than chaos.

Another change is that the pace of progress has changed so drastically that we can no longer forecast that any single economic direction will have enduring worth. In 1862 our leaders saw the great frontier, the westward expansion, the immense resource stores, and the booming metropolitan centers, and recognized that investment in "agricultural and mechanic arts" were going to pay off in the long term for individuals and for the nation. What would we see now as an analogue, as a mode of action or thinking with sufficient payoff to warrant decades of attention?

(No, not STEM. First of all, the category (Science, Technology, Engineering, and Mathematics) is silly. Science and mathematics are not technical, careerist disciplines. They are investigative, speculative, and risky, which is partly why they've declined as a proportion of majors. Technology and engineering are the booming, applied majors that offer reliable expertise for nameable jobs. Second, we've been sloppy in thinking that rigor equals quantification. If we want people to be smart, attentive, disciplined, and rigorous, any kind of work can be the vessel for that; look at a professional dancer, a jazz musician, an elite sprinter, a philosopher, a poet. Third, there are plenty of signs that the STEM pipeline is already overfilled; there's no shortage of technically trained workers.[24] For the most part, STEM is just a lazy way of saying we want people to invent more cool, inexpensive gadgets for us to buy.)

These two forces, individualization and pace of economic change, mean that, although vocational college education persists, it is no longer the stable, patient, stepwise endeavor it once was. Colleges now have to keep up with an economy that changes faster than schools can; students are faced with thousands of career choices they can only faintly understand. We see fields growing and fading on the basis of media attention: the boom in forensics programs tracking the *CSI* television franchise, students choosing fashion design influenced by their love of cable shows like *Project Runway* and *Say Yes to the Dress*, a sudden swell in medievalists due to HBO's *Game of Thrones*. We see colleges modifying curricula to suit manufacturers' needs.[25] Savvy students are encouraged to choose their majors with one eye on the various prognostications of fastest-growing jobs—audiologist? cost estimator? event planner?—betting now against some speculator's odds on the future. It's worth noting that in the 1960s and early '70s it was widely predicted that college faculty would be a gigantic growth area; that missed prediction is part of why this book exists.

College is less often thought of as a public good, and increasingly seen as an individual investment in an individual career, one that individuals borrow against in the hope of personal dividends. From this point of view, the phrase "So what are you going to do with *that*?" is not crass or gauche. It reflects the instrumental view of knowledge that most people have. Knowledge, in that view, is a tool that allows you to do certain things. A major in engineering or nursing or business or education is a named tool; we know there's a bolt out there in the world that wrench will fit. A major in philosophy, mathematics, anthropology, physics, music, geography . . . well, what can you do with that?

We can see the proportional changes when we look at degrees

conferred over the past forty years.[26] The classic liberal arts majors—English, languages, sciences, mathematics, social sciences—have all declined in percentages of baccalaureate degrees conferred. The big increases have come in career-prep programs:

- computer and information sciences (385 percent increase)
- leisure and fitness studies (340 percent)
- homeland security, law enforcement, and firefighting (147 percent)
- communications and journalism (116 percent)
- communications technologies (100 percent)
- health professions (83 percent).

The elite colleges have largely avoided such programs, working as they do with children of privilege who'll do just fine in life regardless of their college major. But in the working-class and middle-class colleges, most of the participants—families, counselors, and students alike—imagine a sort of ballistic model of career planning, in which they aim today at a target they intend to hit after several years. A student decides at some moment that she wants to be an electrical engineer or a nurse, and takes educational and professional steps that will help her become that. There's a goal out there, and students create a path they think will get them successfully and efficiently from where they are to where they want to be. They ready, they aim, and they fire. Often they arrive at a target that isn't what they thought it would be. Often they arrive at a target from which the rewards have moved on to another location. Often they miss the target because of intervening winds. Every shot is a gamble, and individual students rarely get a second try.

All of this focus on individuals and their career-specific preparation has led to a remarkable growth in new degree programs, any of which could be jettisoned if either the career track or the program enrollment doesn't play out as planned. Athletic training and exercise science, sports management and hospitality, cybersecurity and digital forensics, graphic design and new media, entrepreneur-ialism . . . dozens and dozens of new degree tracks have emerged in the pursuit of what seem like potentially fruitful career tracks, just as hundreds of thousands of people followed the Gold Rush or the housing bubble.

These temporary fads are bad for students and for colleges in many ways, but our focus is on how they contribute to contingency in academic employment. The growth of new programs has not been tracked by a growth of TT hiring for at least three reasons. The first is that, being transient and responsive to fluid markets, career-driven programs do not lend themselves to a permanent faculty. It's a safe bet to hire a tenure-track faculty member in physics for a forty-year career; physics will exist in perpetuity. Robotics will not; it may be replaced in twenty or thirty years by a technology we can't begin to imagine today. These new fields are presumed to be ephemeral, chasing trends that can't be fully foreseen, but which we can assume to be fluid. Colleges have no interest in hiring tenured faculty to oversee them.

Second, because career-based majors don't track the historic disciplines, there won't be scholars with PhDs waiting to take those few faculty positions that are created. Most career-based majors aren't scholarly endeavors anyway; they're instrumental, functional, and have no need of critical intellectual apparatus. So those positions will be filled by people who hold master's degrees or less, and who have some professional experience. Career degrees lead toward trade schools, which are more akin to apprenticeship than to academic programs, and which offer no home for the scholar. Put bluntly:

> "We are focused on more career and technical education," said Jeremy Shirley, director of marketing and communications for Arkansas State University Newport. "All of our programs have advisory boards, and we tailor the programs to meet industry needs. That drives a lot of what we do, and our general education and liberal arts exist to supplement those programs."[27]

". . . Our general education and liberal arts exist to supplement those programs." That's just a radically different understanding of the nature of college than would be expressed at Stanford, Yale, or Oberlin. We can thank Mr. Shirley for stating the case so clearly; one can only hope that all colleges could name their core purposes as well.

Third and finally, these career-prep fields have raised important questions about the nature and necessity of degrees. If an employer really just wants a lab technician, why should she take any interest in her potential employee's understanding of sociology or literature, or his ability to write a critical essay or understand physics? What she wants is someone who understands the use of specific equipment, follows specific procedures, upholds specific safety and quality protocols, makes rapid decisions when faced with new circumstances, and doesn't embarrass the company when he sends an email. Half a dozen courses will achieve all of that; no need for the other thirty-four.

> Badges can represent different levels of work and engagement, including more granular skills or achievements, marking in some cases small and/or very specific abilities. For this reason badges hold particular promise for certifying the skills of adult learners in basic education programs, many of whom have few, if any, formal credentials (such as diplomas), but who are obtaining functional skills that would be valued in a workplace setting if a mechanism for certifying those skills and knowledge was available.[28]

There's an increasing shift toward badges and certificates that name demonstrated competency in discrete tasks, each individual job seeker able to show off dozens of badges like a Girl Scout. The job applicant waves her smartphone at her interviewer's videocam, and he can see her badges in résumé and cover letter preparation; in writing for social media; and in professional correspondence, emails, and memos. This granularity of knowledge will by necessity be matched by a granularity of courses and course providers, the carefully curated curriculum replaced by an individualized accumulation of skill bits.

The shift away from the historic disciplines to a new array of career preparatory fields makes contingency almost inevitable. It eliminates the permanence of academic careers, the stability of academic disciplines, and the need for critical scholarly preparation. It is the "app-ing" of higher education. The affluent professional and executive colleges face no such pressures, and their stability accrues to student and faculty alike.

LABOR-INTENSIVE . . . BUT WHAT KIND OF LABOR?

> I'm struck by how many of my cohort thought they were headed for junior faculty, who've become data managers or advocates for women in science or some nonteaching role. There were a few of my colleagues who wound up running academic programs, like a travel study program. An associated thing that wasn't what they'd set out to do.
>
> —Paul, adjunct faculty member for ten years

As always, the wealthy become wealthier, and those with little to start with are provided with the least. But as intriguing as the income side of the question is, let's have a look at the expense side.

As much as we might be seduced by the idea of giant online schools, MOOCs (Massively Open Online Courses) with fifty thousand students and one teacher, most of higher education is still a close-contact endeavor, with some number of young humans in a room with a somewhat older human, discussing ideas. Good teaching and learning have always been labor-intensive processes. As one of my correspondents, a provost at an elite undergraduate college, said, "When the movement to MOOCs was at its rabid peak a couple of years ago and some members of our board were talking about starting to do more distance education, I regularly told them that at our school, distance education is the length of a table."

What we've seen in recent years, though, is that the labor-intensive nature of education hasn't increased educational staffing, but rather

TABLE 5   Overall staffing per thousand students, 2000 to 2012

	Research universities		Master's universities		Bachelor's colleges		Community colleges
	Public	Private	Public	Private	Public	Private	Public
2000	317	434	172	216	184	262	191
2012	301	456	172	243	184	277	175
% change	−5%	+5%	—	+12%	—	+6%	−8%

Source: Desrochers and Kirshstein, "Labor Intensive or Labor Expensive?"

professional positions in finance, operations, admissions, financial aid, information technology, academic counseling, health care, and fundraising. The American Institutes for Research (AIR) showed that "professional positions increased, on average, by 2.5 to 5 percent per year between 2000 and 2012. . . . Professional workers now account for approximately 20 to 25 percent of on-campus jobs."[29]

Again, categories are somewhat variable, but table 5 shows AIR's quick look at staffing changes at different kinds of schools. The numbers are expressed in employees per thousand students. Private colleges have allowed tuition to rise enough (and their investments have done well enough) to add staff at all educational levels, whereas tax funding cuts in public schools have resulted in flat staffing at middle-class schools, and reduced funding at both ends of the spectrum, the executive state research schools and the working-class community colleges. When combined with the substantial growth in non-academic professional staff, as the business of higher education becomes increasingly complex, we can easily see the pressures that are being placed upon faculty hiring.

HUNTING EXPEDITIONS: STUDENT RECRUITMENT AND ENDOWMENT DEVELOPMENT

As student numbers become unpredictable and state appropriations less generous, institutions are on the perpetual hunt for new sources of revenue, an excursion that looks different at different kinds of schools. Working-class and middle-class schools have active college-employer partnerships, brainstorming new ways to fill local business needs. The state and federal departments of education love this stuff, seeing education primarily as a form of "workforce development."

> Over just the past four years, this Administration has invested approximately $2 billion for 700 community colleges to partner with employers to design education and training programs that prepare workers for jobs that are in-demand in their regional economies, such as health care, information technology, and energy. These programs are promising—by the end of 2014, more than 1,900 new or modified training programs had been launched.
> —US Department of Education press release, 2016[30]

Middle-class four-year schools do this as well, but they also have other options. They add degree levels, attracting those earnest and willing enough to spend another two or three years to prove their capability (and who've discovered that a bachelor's degree no longer serves to differentiate them from the great herd of workers, since more than a third of all adults between twenty-five and twenty-nine years old have undergraduate degrees).[31] This is what lies behind so many state schools changing their names from "college" to "university" in recent years: a university has graduate programs, and graduate programs are on the rise. The percentage of young adults with master's degrees or higher has doubled in the past twenty years, to more now than 10 percent.[32]

Every couple of weeks, *Inside Higher Ed* publishes a column of new programs announced by colleges around the country. In just the first quarter of 2017, this accounted for thirty-nine new programs. More than half were at the master's level, the new bubble economy in higher ed that colleges have developed after running undergraduate learning (and lending) to its limits:

- one certificate program, in automotive service management
- three associate's programs, in graphic design, information security and intelligence, and 3-D graphics technology

- eleven baccalaureate programs, in agricultural business, public health (two), business and technology of fashion, oceanography, criminology and criminal justice, health sciences, risk management and insurance, digital marketing management, health professions, and behavioral neuroscience
- twenty-one master's programs in global and community health, justice studies, business analytics, heritage studies and public history, cybersecurity risk management, psychology (online), sustainable development, business analytics, applied child and adolescent development (two, one online), genetic counseling, fashion design, engineering entrepreneurship, leadership, management, accounting, communication media arts, cyberphysical systems, operations management, film studies, and trans-Atlantic affairs.
- three doctoral programs: two EdD's in higher education leadership (online) and health professions, and one PhD in creative writing in Spanish.

These new programs require not merely teachers but also coordinative staff, admissions recruiters, advising staff, graphic materials, and advertising. They place increased demands on the financial aid and registrar's offices.

Middle-class state colleges have also worked hard to attract more out-of-state and international students who pay higher tuition, usually two or three times the in-state rate. This places every school into a marketing race, with more pressure to be consumer-attractive; all those stereotypical climbing walls and food courts are the outcomes of students thinking about any college anywhere as a viable alternative. Colleges are forced to advertise themselves on the most basic levels: *If our curriculum is the same as everyone else's, and our faculty are the same as everyone else's, maybe our smoothie bar will win the day*. It also creates pressure to increase recruitment expenses and add admissions representatives, salespeople charged with maintaining or increasing their individual school's enrollment from the shrinking pool of potential students.

Affluent professionals' schools have added a few master's programs here and there, but are mostly willing to let tuition be the floating variable—attracting, as they always have, the children of comfort and leisure. And they have conducted massive fundraising campaigns, their comfortable and loyal alumni responsive to requests for further endowing the dear alma mater. Williams College, Boston College, and Amherst College are all in the two-billion-dollar endowment club; take the threshold down to a mere billion and we add Pomona, Wellesley, Swarthmore, Grinnell, Smith, Bowdoin, Berea, and Middlebury.[33]

Seeing the success of their betters, colleges of all sorts have thrown seed money into offices of development or advancement, cultivating prospective donors and writing funding proposals for new programs. They've also opened offices of sponsored research, a second team working to help faculty write grant proposals and manage awards. These two projects do not merely represent more staff; even if they're successful (and they often don't make their own money back), they act as a further engine toward churn and complexity. Colleges often imagine that advancement income and research funding represent "free money," but such gifts themselves are forces of contingency.

It's always possible to spend more money to pursue the quality of education, so schools are perpetually proposing new programs and then scrambling to pay for them. Fortunately, there is no end of people and agencies willing to support these initiatives . . . kind of. These generous souls, whether individual donors or family funds or major foundations or federal agencies, have social goals of their own; they're giving money to some college in order to further their own complex missions. Every negotiation over a grant or a gift becomes an imperfect alignment of values. Without constant attention and focus, the college can be distracted from its core mission through the necessity of fundraising, each new initiative making it a little different than it once had been. After ten or twenty or fifty years, the school becomes unrecognizable.

In the for-profit world, this doesn't matter even a little bit. The executives of US Steel, when asked in the 1980s how they could continue to make steel in the face of so many plant closures, replied, "We don't make steel. We make money."[34] There's no complex array of core values there, just dollars. So it's easy for them to divest from one area and pick up another, to shift from sheet metal to structural steel to iron mining. McDonald's doesn't make hamburgers, they make money. They'll sell McNuggets and Fruit 'n Yogurt Parfait and McCafé Shamrock Chocolate Chip Frappé. Maybe next year they'll sell McPhones and McSoap and McGin 'n Tonic. Money has no mission except its own.

In our contemporary zeal to "run government like a business," colleges have invested in the fluid, the entrepreneurial, the venture capital environment in which we throw a lot of projects at the wall to see what sticks. Each new program on its own makes a lot of sense; as a portfolio of programs, as a system of programs, they change the school irretrievably. We build the entrepreneurial university, and then wonder why everyone is so overworked and confused about the mission. We fret about the churn that we ourselves have caused.

Along with simple gifts, schools have raised expectations for research and scholarly productivity, in the hopes of attracting research grant funding and industry research-and-development partnerships like the big dogs. Just like college football, though, college research is almost always a money loser for all but a tiny handful of universities. The NCAA shows that only twenty-four universities actually had football programs that were profit centers for their schools; on average, 20 percent of the cost of running even elite, Bowl-eligible football programs were paid out of university expenses.[35] The hope, often untested, is that the support of football pays off in other ways, through recruitment, branding, and the loyalty and generosity of alumni.

Research funding is much the same: an attempt at striving, at having the public face of a university. And, like football, funded research typically doesn't directly cover its own expenses except at the very, very most successful universities. The former president of Ohio State, Karen Holbrook, wrote in 2014, "There is a significant gap between the real costs of university research and the funding that is available to support university research. Greater administrative financial support is needed for investigators and new, external funding sources need to be explored to pay for indirect costs, such as staff, equipment, educational resources, and travel."[36] It turns out to cost a lot of money to raise a golden goose.

Every new initiative, regardless of its funding source or its ultimate success, changes all the other parts of the ecosystem. There are new committees and coordinative challenges. There are requirements for space and equipment, demands placed on accounting and human resources. There are course releases to fill, travel and memberships to fund. And at the end of the project, questions of permanence: Is this thing valuable enough for us to continue it with our own funding? Does it become a new member of the community, or does it migrate through us and then depart? How far did we stray from our mission to bring it on board?

These programs also add to the impermanence of the higher-education workplace. A school gets a three-year grant, and adds "soft-money employees" and a few postdocs who can be shed without regrets when the funding dries up. The permanent faculty member gets the glory (in promotion credit, and in publications and reputation); the others get to not be hungry for a little while longer while they do their temp jobs with one eye on the classified ads. A college gets to advertise its new master's degree program, not putting out similar press releases when that program closes after five years, leaving its adjunct faculty without a market for the courses they've relied upon teaching.

NOT MERELY MORE STUDENTS, BUT MORE DIVERSE

. . . Students organized a march around campus and presented administrators with their demands. They want five new counselors for the coming academic year, with three of them being people of color, "to reflect the increasing need of health and wellness initiatives at Mudd [Harvey Mudd College] to reflect and serve its diversifying student body," the students wrote on a website detailing their requests. Funding for mental health services should be boosted every year by 25 percent, they wrote, until the 2021–22 academic year. They called for a release of the student affairs office's budget, and additional money—$3,000 each—for six student groups that represent minority interests on campus. The administration also should carve out dedicated spaces in the college's new academic building for each of these six groups, they wrote.

    —Jeremy Bauer-Wolf, "Harvey Mudd Cancels Classes."[37]

The myth of the stable college drew on a historical truth: the enterprise was founded on a legacy of comfortable old guys teaching comfortable young guys. Part of that comfort was financial, part of it was paternalistic, and part of it was ethnic. It's only been in relatively recent times that women, people of color, the LGBTQ+ community, international citizens, and other nonwhite, nonmale, nonstraight, nonnative students have made up the collective majority of the undergraduate population.

It's no surprise that a habitat historically self-selecting for white maleness hasn't easily fit a more diverse community.[38] And that misfit often isn't intentional as much as it is confused, a surprised and well-intentioned realization: "Oh, everybody isn't like me? Gosh, let me fix something!" The fixes often come from the top, from faculty and administrative committees, and so aren't very responsive to the real conditions students experience. They're often hasty, especially since the undergrads most affected by them will be the most transient members of the community, and anything that's going to help a sophomore have an improved college experience had better be implemented in a year or less. And they're often reluctant, since the established members of the community are familiar with what they have and what they know, and believe it to not only be normal but proper. Just acknowledging privileges is never easy or comfortable, let alone releasing some of them.

But over fifty years or so, the changes have come, slowly and incrementally. Some of them are federally mandated: the Title III, Title

IX, and TRIO programs that have worked to support the college success of women, first-generation students, adult reengagement students, and people of color. Some of them are local and informal: the development of a Latinx group, a women's professional-mentoring network, or a "safe space" program for queer youth to find comfortable mentors. Some of them are broadly shared but locally specific: the widespread adoption of the various high-impact educational practices, like undergraduate research, first-year learning communities, and community-based education, that have been demonstrated to contribute to student engagement and student success.[39]

As a result, colleges have opened new offices that focus on specialized areas of student support—academic, social, and emotional. More than seven hundred colleges are institutional members of the Council on Undergraduate Research (CUR), for instance, and many of these schools have a formal office of undergraduate research on their campuses; one of the fastest growing divisions in CUR has been the group made up of undergraduate research program directors. More than a thousand colleges are members of Campus Compact, an organization dedicated to learning within the context of service to one's surrounding community. Coordinators of first-year experience, directors of service learning, internship placement offices, writing across the curriculum programs, honors programs, women's centers—the list is endless.[40] One common tactic of professional organizations is to call for the development of "an office of . . ." to address their favored issue, and to indicate institutional buy-in. The Campus Compact website puts it plainly: "One of the clearest signs that an idea is valued on campus is that it has its own office."[41]

Student advising is nothing like its earlier iterations; it now proliferates with international student support, English as a Second Language staff, learning disabilities specialists, and programs for students with eating disorders and body dysmorphia. It has been estimated that more than 10 percent of all of America's college students are single mothers, and in response, working-class and middle-class colleges are increasingly in the child care business as well.[42]

A significant body of research has found that the positive impacts of student service expenditures are greatest at working-class and middle-class institutions with the most at-risk student populations, as measured by higher Pell Grants and lower entrance test scores.[43] The National Center for Developmental Education notes that remedial education should be only one component of a larger student support network that addresses emotional resiliency, food and housing security, health care, legal aid, and other common barriers to college success.[44] It's relatively easy to teach economically comfortable, academically prepared students who are all between the ages of eighteen and twenty-two; it's the working-class and middle-class schools that have had the greatest growth in academic and student services, even as their overall funding is deeply uncertain.

These powerful and productive responses to the increasing diversity of the student body have simultaneously and unintentionally contributed to the growth of contingent faculty. The American Institutes for Research has found that just between 2003 and 2013, spending on both student services and academic support has grown far more rapidly than spending on instruction.[45] These professionals individually cost roughly as much in salary and benefits as early-career faculty, so it's close to being a one-to-one question: Do we hire a faculty member in physics, math, or anthropology? Or do we hire a director of writing across the curriculum? Or a director of international student engagement? Or a director for our Asian American Cultural Center? Or a new mental health counselor? Which one will we, as a college, be most likely to see benefit from? Which one are we likely to get at least partial funding for? Which one are we going to be stuck with forever, even if the winds shift?

These initiatives of contemporary higher ed work both for and against students, because it's almost certain that the enormous contingent faculty won't be welcome to participate in any of them. Adjuncts won't be invited to the professional development workshops about community-engaged learning, won't be invited to include their students as research partners in their (unfunded and often nonexistent) scholarly endeavors. They won't be paid to attend safe-space training for LGBTQ+ support, or to attend workshops about

support for autistic students. They won't even know the array of resources available to students on their campuses.[46]

In this way, all of these programs work at cross-purposes, simultaneously serving and undermining the students of the working-
class and middle-class schools. The lower tier of schools will have
a small proportion of faculty involved in high-impact practices and
trained in student support, because they have fewer TT faculty in
whom they're willing to invest. All of these contemporary academic
and support practices are based in student engagement, in helping
young people feel as though they personally belong in the intellectual world; they work in large part because they promote close one-
on-one relationships between students and faculty. We undercut
our own best intentions by having such a large proportion of faculty
with whom students can build no such connections.[47]

The paradox is that almost all these services were once offered
by the faculty themselves, and still largely are offered by faculty at
the affluent schools. Each of the various high-impact practices was
developed by faculty in the course of doing their day-to-day work.
Counseling of students in difficulty was done in faculty offices. Academic advising, the setting of a student's path through the garden of
ideas, was done by individual faculty members. But these practices
were unique and idiosyncratic, weren't developed to serve a more
diverse student community, and weren't equipped to keep pace with
the regulatory details of state and federal oversight (we'll talk more
about that next). Specialization arose to meet the greater complexity
of student needs and a broader array of opportunities, and specialization means specialized employees—lots and lots of specialized
employees.

EVERY MOVE YOU MAKE: THE COSTS OF COMPLIANCE

Each summer, higher education lawyers gather at the annual conference of the National Association of College and University Attorneys (NACUA) to hear speakers and discuss topics relevant to our
institutions. The meeting is also a chance for networking and can-

did conversations with others confronting similar challenges. The annual conference program, together with NACUA's biannual survey of chief legal officers, provides insight into the issues that keep your lawyers up at night.[48]

The Higher Education Compliance Alliance works to maintain an updated guide to federal laws that carry consequences for colleges and universities. This guide, which they call the Compliance Matrix, represents an astonishing array of ways in which a school can screw up.[49] There are thirty-one different categories of college practices accounted for, from academic programs to environmental health and occupational safety to human resources to sexual misconduct. Each category is ruled by at least one federal regulation, and as many as thirteen (information technology), twenty-four (financial aid), or forty (human resources).

It's not reasonable to expect every faculty member to be up to speed on Title III, Title IX, the Americans with Disabilities Act, and the Clery Act. And those are the big ones: colleges are also responsible for compliance with the Campus Sex Crimes Prevention Act, the Davis-Bacon Act, the Trading with the Enemy Act, the Lilly Ledbetter Fair Pay Act, the Chemical Facility Anti-Terrorism Standards, the Small Unmanned Aircraft Systems regulations, and hundreds of others. Many of these laws carry annual reporting requirements; all of them are subject to procedural or record audits at least, along with possible fines and prohibitions if violations are uncovered. The regulatory environment leads to its own specialization in the accounting, legal and financial aid, and student services groups — more nonfaculty personnel who displace faculty hiring.

Let me be understood properly. I believe the increasing diversity of the college student community is good. The support we offer to foster student success, to not just dump freshmen into class and hope they can hack it, is good. The increasing oversight that prevents schools from shirking their human and financial and social responsibilities is good. But all those good things cost money and require staffing, and are increasingly seen as higher-ed requirements in a way that permanent faculty are not. The growth of contingency is sped forward by an accumulation of unintended consequences.

FLUID MISSION: UNSETTLED FACULTY

This is higher education in the twenty-first century. Colleges enroll an ever greater proportion of the young, and thus are subject to demographic swings that leave each semester's enrollments uncertain until opening day. Individual students are mobile and impermanent, shifting from school to school and from state to state. Collectively, the student body is far more diverse along every possible trait, and demands staffing that responds to vast differences in life circumstances that simply didn't exist in colleges half a century ago.

The labor market is unpredictable, changing rapidly, its skills increasingly thought to be disaggregated and granular; schools respond by creating a wider variety of impermanent, career-chasing programs. The funding structure and the product mix are also changing constantly, with new programs and new degree levels in an attempt to supplant funding formerly drawn from stable and reliable legislative contributions.

Colleges are asked to do more and more, and have done so admirably. But everybody involved in the enterprise is hindered by the density of interconnection, the fact that every decision has implications for dozens or hundreds of other offices on campus. Financial aid is a vast enterprise, answering to federal oversight and private lenders and endowment managers; every college now contains the equivalent of a small-town bank. Multidevice computing, wireless connectivity, learning-management systems, and building-efficiency protocols didn't exist when I went off to college; neither did offices of undergraduate research, service learning, community engagement, or women's centers. Every decision that might be made requires more bodies at the table, an exponential growth in meetings and email, and a more delicate balance between competing benefits—every interaction a game of Jenga that might collapse without warning.

The college of 1976 would be deemed indefensibly underequipped in the contemporary higher education environment, just as a 1976 Oldsmobile Cutlass would be less reliable, less efficient, and less safe than any car currently available. We can be nostalgic, but the modern college is a far more sophisticated environment than its predecessors, serving a larger and more diverse student community. That sophistication itself has resulted in rebalancing of the populations; the contingent community has grown larger and weaker in response.

6

THE COMFORTS OF THOSE
INSIDE THE CASTLE

The world of the student is filled with mechanisms for identifying and rewarding talent: talent on certain terms, of course, but talent nonetheless. We pack thirty kindergarten kids into a room and ask them all to do the same thing. Some will do it better than others. We repeat that dozens of times a day, 180 days a year for thirteen years, and we have a relatively effective means of identifying who can do the things we value.

The ones who do those things well—the gold that remains in the pan—get to do them some more; they get higher-level tasks that require greater focus and more sophistication. The machine winnows yet again for another four or five years of college, and a few of those participants are invited to continue even further, to graduate school, for another five or more years of the same.

In every case the machine is designed, like a quiz show, to continually feed its participants challenges at which they can identifiably do better or worse. It is a virtual reality, a protective pod that seems like the whole world but is actually an illusion. We don't recognize it in the moment, because it seems so real—we're immersed within its structures, it gives us the positive feedback that we crave, and it rewards the odd blend of curiosity and obedience that we have cultivated so carefully.

But ultimately the day comes when we have passed all of those challenges, and there is no more machine feeding us, challenging us, praising us. There is only the vast, incoherent, airless ether of "the job market."

The market rewards what it rewards, in a peculiar, circular, unknowable fashion. There is no conceivable explanation for why more people like Justin Timberlake's music than Kaki King's, except that they do. There is no conceivable explanation for why more people have read Nicholas Sparks than Jennifer Tseng, except that they have. The matrix—the logical, structured system of challenges and rewards—has finished with us, and we have entered an entirely different logic system, one we were never informed of. One that will comfortably dispose of the majority of us.

In the market, the tasks are less structured, the opportunities for challenge are less frequent, the feedback less defined. Instead of a dozen papers a year to write for professors whom students have come to know, doctoral graduates now have cover letters to write for the three jobs a year in their field, written to people who are anonymous, who do not themselves know what they want—letters that will receive no feedback of any sort, aside from "No, thank you."

Those few who manage somehow to cross that wilderness will, surprisingly, reenter the matrix. They will once again be given specific tasks in a reliable sequence—creating and teaching courses, conducting and submitting research, serving on committees and preparing for promotion. They will get regular feedback, and thus be able to learn, to reenergize the paired muscles of curiosity and obedience. They will be welcomed back into to the pod, the virtual reality, the loving arms of the mechanical mother. They will, in fact, now help to shape it. And they will forget the terrors of the space between.

We can't discuss the contingent faculty without also talking about those, fewer in number and greater in power, who are permanently employed to provide and oversee the education of our students. Why have both faculty and administrators been so ineffective in the nurturance and defense of their intellectual colleagues? Why has it been so easy to dismiss the millions of fallen?

THE TT FACULTY: I GOT MINE, TOO BAD ABOUT YOU

There are hundreds of thousands of tenure-track faculty, endangered but still not extinct. And each one of them has every reason to believe that she or he made it because of merit, because she did something right or because all the others did something wrong. There's a strong hindsight bias that works to confirm one's own positive traits, whether those traits are skill, talent, hard work, or persistence. And the nation's faculty, as a whole, *are* enormously skilled, talented, hardworking, and persistent. Those are necessary traits. The question is whether the TT faculty hold those traits in greater proportion and degree than the much larger community of NTT who could rise up to replace them.

Both Robert Frank and Malcolm Gladwell have written marvelously about opportunity, the necessary third ingredient that, when mixed with talent and work, produces success.[1] But when successful people don't acknowledge the role that things outside their control have played in their success, they don't think to create those conditions for others; they imagine that the less fortunate are simply less worthy.

In a charmingly frank post on his *Inside Higher Ed* blog, community college dean Matt Reed discusses some of the unseen elements that go into his decision to make a faculty hire.[2] First, the presence of adjuncts reduces the likelihood of creating a TT position (or "line").

> In a particularly cruel catch-22, the relative ease of finding adjuncts for a given discipline actually mitigates against its getting a line. If you can only afford to hire one full-timer, and you have requests from both history and, say, pharmacy, what do you do? If good history adjuncts are easy to find, and good pharmacy adjuncts are nearly impossible, you give the line to pharmacy.

Reed goes on to discuss the ways in which hiring responds to student enrollment patterns, declining funding levels, and the elusive "fit," a sense that the candidate both solves an institution's pressing problems and works to move a department productively forward.

> Sometimes a department needs a peacemaker and sometimes it needs a sparkplug. Sometimes it needs to diversify its demographics by race or gender. Sometimes it's too inbred, with everybody coming from the same one or two graduate programs, and it needs new perspectives. Sometimes it just needs someone who isn't allergic to the internet. None of those has anything to do with "merit" in the sense the term is usually used, but each makes sense in its own way.

The problem is that, once inside the TT gates, the job holder is inside forever, even as the institution's needs change. The fact of tenure increases the stakes for scholars, and increases the ability of those safely ashore to see themselves as winners of a fair competition. A new assistant professor has the first six years of her or his time as a faculty member to demonstrate intellectual capability as a scholar and a teacher; it's a probationary period of sorts. At the end of those six years, the young faculty member goes through a rigorous review by colleagues from the department, from across the college, perhaps even from far-flung members of her or his discipline. Upon successful review, the assistant professor is promoted to become associate professor. This promotion carries with it a significant salary increase, and the guarantee of employment in that position (tenure) until retirement, except in instances of gross malfeasance by the faculty member or a deep financial crisis of the institution.

The underlying idea of tenure, expressed in the American Association of University Professors' 1940 Statement of Principles on Academic Freedom and Tenure, is this:

> Freedom in research is fundamental to the advancement of truth. Academic freedom in its teaching aspect is fundamental for the pro-

tection of the rights of the teacher in teaching and of the student to freedom in learning. . . . Tenure is a means to certain ends; specifically: (1) freedom of teaching and research and of extramural activities, and (2) a sufficient degree of economic security to make the profession attractive to men and women of ability. Freedom and economic security, hence, tenure, are indispensable to the success of an institution in fulfilling its obligations to its students and to society.[3]

Proponents of tenure point to clause 1, the academic freedom that comes from not having to worry about whether unpopular ideas will get them fired. Detractors of tenure point to clause 2, and wonder why anybody anywhere should have a job in perpetuity.[4] And the fact is that clause 2 is kind of snuck in there; nowhere else in the high-minded ideals of the AAUP statement is there any discussion of the economic security of the faculty, and its precursor statement from 1915 refers to job security only in regard to the safety to express unpopular thought and findings, not to economic well-being. The post-Depression fears of unemployment are an add-on rooted in a time of scarcity, when only 4 percent of the adult population even had bachelor's degrees and "attracting men and women of ability" was a mighty problem, a problem that has long since evaporated. Men and women of ability now abound, mostly outside the safe harbors of TT employment.

GHOST IN THE HALLWAYS: THE INSTITUTIONAL INVISIBILITY OF THE CONTINGENT

Until about fifteen years ago, there was no part-time representation on either the faculty senate or the faculty council. The English department invites PTLs to curricular meetings, seminars, social events, but not to department meetings where promotion and tenure and hiring conversations might occur. I mean, there are 255 of us and 55 of them.
—Annette, forty-year adjunct

Adjuncts are invisible to most faculty. Contingent workers aren't paid to come to meetings, and don't have much time for them anyway, so even those rare schools or departments that open larger discussions to their adjuncts don't get a lot of participation. (Which, of course, can be seen by the TTs as further evidence of adjuncts' lack of interest.)

But the larger fact is that even the TT faculty are largely invisible to one another in the details of their daily work. In part because everyone's busy, and in part because of the culture of academic freedom, it's extraordinarily uncommon to have one faculty member sitting in on another's classroom; when it does happen, it's usually a chair or a dean exercising oversight, rather than a colleague exercising curiosity about what's going on in those other classes. Teaching is an isolative culture, one that reveres but rarely explores exactly what happens in the sealed box of a classroom.

Even for TT faculty, the structures of tenure mean that all of a scholar's departmental colleagues look at her written, published work in great detail after a few years as they consider the offer of tenure, and then one more time a few years later to consider her promotion from associate to full professor. That's it. Twice in a career. For adjuncts, there's even less support for or interest in their research lives, so the only thing that gets reviewed are end-of-semester course evaluations, and those only by the department chair.

This makes the work of the lowly NTTs doubly invisible to the TT peerage. It is invisible first because, as with all faculty, no one knows what their teaching or research looks like. And it is invisible a second time because the contingent don't have a role in the larger institutional, departmental, or faculty senate structures.

THE DIVIDED LOYALTIES OF THE ADMINISTRATOR

The traditional role of shared governance in higher education is simple: the faculty and the administration have purview over different aspects of operation. Faculty, individually and collectively, set the curriculum, set the academic standards for students and for colleagues, and set the scholarly agenda for the institution. If the problem is intellectual in nature, the faculty own it. Administrators, on the other hand, raise and allocate resources—resources of time, space, people, and dollars.

It's a commonplace to hear faculty say about one of their colleagues who's become a dean that she's "gone over to the dark side," as though Darth Vader and Luke Skywalker were reasonable analogues for good-natured people trying to collectively manage a school. I'd like to plant a flag in the sand here and reject the "evil administrator" model of explanation for the growth in contingency. Most administrators were faculty members themselves not so long ago; it's unlikely that they've been recruited by some secretive managerial empire to become double agents. There are no distant shareholders demanding that the local branch managers hold wages down so that dividends climb. Again, let's think about it in terms of ecosystems, roles, and adaptation.

Academic management constitutes its own discipline, with its own body of knowledge, its own membership communities and networks, its own journals and conferences. Just as sociologists go to sociology meetings, deans and provosts go to academic administration meetings; just as sociologists borrow the best thinking of their colleagues, deans and provosts borrow "best practices" from their peer institutions. When they come back, they bring invasive species along with them, ideas that are beautiful somewhere else and might make their own landscape more attractive as well. Sometimes the imports don't take: the soil's not right or the climate's too cold. But sometimes the new ideas overcompete and crowd out a lot of previously productive member species. After all, the administrators control resources; if they have a pet idea, it's going to get fertilized. This builds a sameness that renders our thousands of working-class and middle-class colleges redundant except for local convenience and basketball rivalries.

Q: How many faculty members does it take to change a light bulb?

A: CHANGE?!?—Keenan, academic services professional, lower-tier state college

Administrators face the demands for rapid change in ways that the faculty do not. Let's say that a school determines that its students don't do very well with quantitative work. Its provost could ask her faculty to develop a math-across-the-curriculum (MAC) program, which will take six contentious years and result in new names for existing practices. Or she might staff an office of MAC, hire a new coordinator, and get it moving in two years, the rapid progress demonstrating both goodwill and action. The glacial pace of faculty deliberation makes the more definitive actions of administrative structures appealing.

Every faculty member I've ever met rolls their eyes in reflexive response to the words "faculty meeting." Faculty meetings are inevitably miserable affairs. But why? It's simple. Scholars have made their entire careers out of finding problems within what is perceived to be settled knowledge. They carve out that one tiny bubble at the edge of what we know, and they focus all of their ample energies and intelligence on precisely defining, or redefining, or complicating that small issue.

Gather a hundred of these people together, and give them a policy to review. You think that's going to go well? The 90 percent of the policy that everyone could agree on will go unremarked. Instead, each participant will focus on one unseen problem, one awkward phrase, one unacknowledged conflict. Soon, with everybody tugging at their one favorite thread, the whole fabric comes unraveled. Faculty earn their reputations as arrogant nitpickers because that's the core trait that makes them faculty! They've been trained for decades to find a flaw or gap in thinking, and to state with some degree of confidence that they've analyzed it properly and proposed the appropriate resolution. Faculty governance takes the very best attributes of scholars and employs them in the very worst ways. It's no wonder that administrators, under different time pressures, try to bypass that in order to get some work done.

Administrators also represent a culture different from that of their faculty friends, a culture marked by divided attention. They have to have their eyes on dozens of departments, dozens of campus initiatives, an array of dumpster fires to be extinguished before the day can even begin. When I was a dean, I was paid to be interrupted; most of my work was coordinative rather than individually productive. Academics and administrators speak different languages of time. Scholars need chunks of unbroken time: hours in the lab, hours in front of the word processor, months away in the field. The ceaseless flow of minute-to-minute pressures causes administrators to forget that, and leads them to think that everybody is available all the time for coordinative meetings, reporting, and responding to emails and requests for assessment data. The simplest way to think of it is that meetings *are* the work of administrators; meetings *prevent* the work of faculty.

> There's nothing so dangerous as a dean just back from a conference.
> —Harry, dean, middle-class state college

Because of their broad array of responsibilities, administrators are part of many more professional societies than any of their faculty colleagues. They attend conferences of state and regional associations, organizations of schools with related missions—Catholic colleges, liberal arts colleges, schools of art and design, law schools, graduate schools. They attend meetings of organizations that promote particular learning structures—service learning, first-year seminars, metacognitive reflection, capstone projects. They attend meetings held by their various accrediting bodies. And they attend meetings that help them to be better at their own work of coordination and persuasion and financial management. Any one dean will travel to more meetings than any six faculty members; this costs money and carries with it all the common dangers of promiscuity, ideas that spread uncontrolled to new partners.

Because of the increased scale and breadth of the higher-ed enterprise, those charged with its oversight have an increasingly dense, interwoven managerial task. As a result, executive compensation has increased, and seven-figure college president salaries, though still uncommon, are no longer rare. (In thirty-nine states, the highest-paid public employee is the coach of a college basketball or football team.[5] When an academic employee is highest paid, it's as likely to be the dean of a medical school as a university president.) Although executive salaries pale in comparison with the cost of an Aramark contract or experimental equipment, there's still something galling for contingent workers scolded about the necessity of cost-cutting by someone whose compensation might outscale theirs by twenty to one.

Whether their pay is or isn't warranted, though, senior administrators have a tough job, and often manage their constantly changing demands by collaborating as much with partners outside their colleges as they do within, by aligning themselves with professional and legislative standards. In this way, they reduce the uniqueness of individual colleges, bringing even more pressure toward trivial rather than fundamental distinction. The genius of bureaucracy is that it makes genius into bureaucracy, taking bright, risky ideas and burying them inside safe layers of structure. The further we go toward standard practices, the sooner the Amazon.com of higher education is coming.

THE UNSPOKEN THIRD PARTIES

The invasive species of higher education don't just conceal themselves within the luggage of individual administrators back from their travels; they also attach themselves to host schools through institutional memberships and accreditation standards. Here's a list of institutional memberships for a single middle-class state college:

- Accreditation Board for Engineering and Technology
- American Association for Health Education
- American Chemical Society
- American Council on the Teaching of Foreign Languages
- Association for Childhood Education International
- Aviation Accreditation Board International
- Commission on Accreditation of Allied Health Education Programs

- Commission on Accreditation of Athletic Training Education
- Council for Exceptional Children
- Council on Social Work Education
- Council on Undergraduate Research
- Council for Accreditation of Counseling and Related Educational Programs
- Educational Leadership Constituent Council
- Federal Aviation Administration
- International Reading Association
- International Society for Technology in Education
- Interstate Agreement for Educator Licensure
- National Association for the Education of the Young Child
- National Association of Schools of Music
- National Association of Schools of Art and Design
- National Association of Schools of Public Affairs and Administration
- National Council for the Social Studies
- National Council for the Accreditation of Teacher Education/ Council for the Accreditation of Educator Preparation
- National Council of Teachers of English
- National Council of Teachers of Mathematics
- New England Association of Schools and Colleges
- Society for Health and Physical Educators

Each of these organizations prioritizes normalcy, making sure that the franchises don't get too far away from the home office's operation manual. Each organization has paid permanent staff. Each requires money for memberships and conference travel (the cost of which will not be paid for contingent members of the community, thus further marginalizing adjuncts from their former disciplinary peers).[6] Each requires time for volunteer support and professional participation. Each requires reporting of departmental or institutional practices. Each requires adjustment of local curricula to fit larger interests. Each organization works to promote contingency through increasing the transferability of credits, and through taking institutional money away from teaching (while still placing the expenditures in the opaque budget category of "instruction," thus making them look more benign than they are).

Then add on the state and federal task forces, each making "commonsense requests" that seem individually reasonable but actually mask foundational changes. For instance, the State Council of Higher Education for Virginia has declared that civic engagement is going to be a "core competency" against which all of its member schools will be assessed.[7] Each of the University of North Carolina System's schools is asked to play a role in the economic development of its home county.[8] The Vermont Agency of Education is responsible for implementing the state legislature's Flexible Pathways Initiative, which urges member schools to offer early college or dual-enrollment programs to get high school graduates into college.[9] Each agency works to optimize its unique initiative, leaving individual campuses whipsawed as they attempt to integrate innumerable competing interests.

Higher education is not merely the thousands of visible and accountable colleges around the nation. Higher education is also the thousands and thousands of shadow organizations—professional societies, think tanks, private foundations, legislative partners, and accrediting bodies—each of which employs professional and non-professional staff, puts on conferences and consume travel funds, publishes journals and newsletters, sends out e-mails, and takes up volunteer time from their members. The ticks are feeding well, even as the deer complain of anemia.

THE PROTECTION OF PRIVILEGE

Each of these three stable communities—tenured and tenure-tracked faculty, administrators and managers, and the innumerable symbiont organizations—have every reason to protect their own turf, and to ignore the needs of those beyond the moat. They see uncertainty in funding, and work to maintain their nutrient stream in the context of a declining overall harvest. They have specific agendas to pursue, and can focus mighty attention on those initiatives, even to the detriment of the larger mission.

In addition, hindsight bias is a powerful psychological force. Higher education is a community of highly intelligent, highly motivated, highly productive people who know how hard they've worked, and who are surrounded by others who are similarly capable. The people on the inside, by and large, are worthy of full membership in the community. But it's easy to move quickly from that understanding to an unwarranted opposite statement: the people on the outside are unworthy.

The relative invisibility of contingent workers is a tool for the emotional comfort of the three permanent communities, just as the invisibility of garment workers in Bangladesh makes it possible for us to justify buying a discount shirt. The presumption of others' unworthiness and the ability to keep them out of sight have always been powerful potions that soothe the consciences of the comfortable.

7

HAPLESS BYSTANDERS

I really loved your course. What else do you teach?
—first-year student, to an adjunct who teaches only that one
first-year course and will never be encountered again

It is easy to see the ills done upon the contingent scholars, the castaways who wash ashore. Why should any others care for the rebalancing of populations? Because everyone associated with higher education suffers in some way from its contingency. Some of those injuries are practical and immediately visible; others are cultural and spiritual.

The permanent faculty are forced to run departments with fewer bodies. There are fewer people to do the daily work, to advise students and revise courses or curricula, to marshal the years of work required for an external review. More importantly, the faculty are diminished when there is a widespread perception that they aren't really needed, that they could be replaced with temp workers or online modules at little cost in effectiveness. The very notion of what it means to be a college professor is thrown open to question. Teaching in general is suspect within a transactional consumer culture: "Those who can, do. Those who can't, teach." The development of the majority-temp faculty reinforces the suspicion that college faculty are interchangeable content providers, that pretty much anybody can do it well enough as long as they have a little more knowledge than their students.

Undergraduate students have fewer faculty available to respond to their curiosity outside the constraints of a classroom. There's a way in which being an undergraduate at a great college is like dating; students take a bunch of classes from a bunch of people, and if they're lucky, they find someone who embodies a way of thinking and a way of life that becomes revelatory. Not everyone will be taken by the same teacher's ideas; that's part of why we make people take forty different courses. But if half of the courses are led by impermanent teachers, even the students who fall in love with an adjunct's thinking can never have a second date, can never see a relationship bloom into a new path through the intellectual garden. They might not even be able to see that teacher between classes, as she rushes off to another class session at another school. The possibilities of mentorship are lost when we reduce faculty life to mere instruction.

The great misunderstanding of college is to believe that it's a sequence of classroom experiences. As wonderful as classes can be, this view of college misses more than it hits, leaving aside the necessarily personal nature of intellectual growth. A friend of mine—we'll call him Professor Lewis—was a faculty member in a very small program (never more than five faculty) that grew remarkably in majors during his time there. When he shifted into administrative life, the number of majors in that program dropped down to an amount even below what it was when he'd started. All those students, for all those years, had essentially majored in Professor Lewis; his discipline was attractive to them because it was the vocabulary in which he spoke of his enthusiasms for the world, enthusiasms that they had come to share.

Graduate students also suffer from being exposed to fewer perspectives, having fewer faculty with their own unique take on the question at hand. The TT faculty who remain are immersed in their own research lives, and grad students can be reduced to employees of a single faculty member's projects rather than being introduced to and challenged by a broader array of ideas. At the same time, doctoral students are increasingly aware that even their very best work might not win them a seat at the faculty table; they constantly have to work with one eye on the odds, sustaining the gumption required to do difficult labor in the face of unlikely outcomes. About half of them won't finish.[1] Of those who do persist, a lot of them become disillusioned, and start to see faculty life as relatively undesirable.[2]

Administrators themselves are hindered by the adjunctification of the faculty. Every semester sees another scramble to hire, to fill positions at the last minute as enrollment demands. Presidents and provosts are dragged across the land in the search for funding and institutional partnerships, education now being only a component of what a college has to offer. They have fewer faculty to offer the wonderful initiatives that they keep inventing. They lose the intellectual brakes that harness the engine of consumer thinking, that keep the fantasies of college presidents from becoming new degree programs that burst in the sky like fireworks, only to sparkle into darkness.

Administrators are also hindered when adjunct faculty are not included in larger issues of campus culture, the intellectual and behavioral norms that are established and modified over time. Adjunct faculty, who are reviewed only on their "teaching effectiveness" (for which course evaluations are the single terrible proxy), rather than on a larger spectrum of activity including scholarship and service, have to find that narrow band of balance between support and rigor.[3] This places pressure on adjuncts to "go easy" on plagiarism and other issues of academic integrity, and to provide more and more of students' intellectual framing rather than asking them to demand more of their own creativity and initiative.[4] The irregularity of adjunct engagement also adds difficulty in all forms of student counseling and assistance, including faculty reporting of sexual assault and harassment among students.[5] The contingent faculty just don't have enough daily experience to be familiar with all of the student supports that a college makes available.

Even the growing population of professional support staff, the seeming winners in all of this, have been coerced into helping to eliminate their nonprofessional colleagues, the clerks and secretaries that have been replaced by outsourcing and technology. The professional support staff have been made to accept the sixty- and seventy-hour workweek as a norm, absorbing a vast amount of work within a flat salary that might formerly have fed a second hourly employee working beside them.

With all of these ills done to so many by contingency, why have we not yet risen up? Why does this model of intellectual servitude persist so strongly? Why are all the bystanders unable to act?

Because it looks normal.

Higher education does not stand apart from our larger culture, which offers its own pressures toward contingency. Even if schools intend to stand as institutions of care and deliberation, as counterweights to the sails of commerce, they will still be strained by the storms around them. The contingency of higher education is merely a local example of contingency framed much more broadly.

PROTECTED CONSUMERS, ABANDONED PRODUCERS

Americans are urged to define ourselves in terms of what we can consume, the greatest variety of the newest things at the lowest cost. We are no longer a culture that makes; we are a culture that buys. We stand above all of that messy production, no longer involved in mining or farming, no longer involved in the danger and disease of manufacturing. Making is tedious and slow. Buying is exciting and fast. Making is risky: it might not come out right. Buying is guaranteed: the product is going to look the way it looked on the website, and we'll exact our Yelping one-star revenge when it doesn't. (*Of course* there are Yelp reviews for colleges. One of my favorites, a review of Foothill College in Palo Alto, includes the line, "Any college campus with free parking gets an automatic 4 stars from me!") Making is exhausting and on the clock. Buying is easy, open-all-night, drive-through, 24/7 gratification.

In the past fifty years we have pressured our legislators to add innumerable consumer protections, and simultaneously shed ourselves of innumerable producer protections. The proportion of our workplace that is unionized—that is, of workers who band together for commonwealth—has declined from nearly a third of nonagricultural workers to about ten percent. The fight for the five-day, forty-hour work week seems quaint, only possible in black-and-white newsreels. Again, this is both cause and effect. When unions don't exist, employers have the power to push wages down and hours up as long as someone will take the work. But the underlying attitude— that workers' lives don't matter; that every worker can be replaced by someone with less experience, or by technology, or by someone in a low-wage nation; or that the stability and predictability of wages has no social benefit—has in turn been a driver of the loss of worker collectivity.

Employers have shed workforce or reduced labor costs in innumerable creative ways, but we can define them into a few core strategies that colleges and universities have adopted in their own ways.

1. **Fewer people, longer hours.** Salaried workers at anything approaching a professional income are ineligible for overtime protection, and professional workplaces have responded by adding so much scope to positions that they can't possibly be fulfilled during an eight-hour day or a five-day week. My colleagues in higher ed constantly tell me of fifty-plus-hour weeks as a baseline condition, occasionally peaking to seventy hours and beyond. And that's before the great curse of email, which we can do all evening and all throughout the weekend and not count as work time. Our parents didn't have email—they went home after work, and didn't see it again until the next morning. Contemporary workers are always available, always in touch.

2. **Workers redefined as independent contractors.** Uber doesn't employ its drivers; it enters into a contractual service-provision relationship with them. The drivers provide their own cars, their own fuel, their own insurance, their own smartphones, their own payroll taxes. Uber merely provides advertising for the service as a whole, the app that holds the enterprise together, and piecework pay for

drivers. (And those drivers make almost no money; the average app-service driver makes about $375 a month.)[6] Adjunct faculty are the piecework equivalent in the higher education world, responsible for all of their own workplace expenses, their own employment taxes, their own health care and retirement, and their own computing, software, and phone and office support. Schools may even mandate that adjuncts hold their reported labor below a certain maximum to avoid institutional responsibility for expensive benefits like health care contributions.[7]

3. **De-bundled professional activities and the creation of parapro-fessionals.** How often do you see a doctor, and for how long? It's more likely that you see a physician assistant, or a nurse practi-tioner. Doctor's offices and hospitals are highly staffed with para-professionals and unlicensed assistive personnel, people who work for lower wages to do what once was part of a doctor's or nurse's daily routine. Likewise, at your lawyer's office a bar-certified law-yer will see you and offer legal advice, but the contract language, document preparation, and scheduling of court appearances will be handled by paralegals. Higher education has not directly named its own version of this phenomenon, but has nonetheless created a class of parafaculty who now conduct the majority of college class-rooms with none of the greater responsibilities or opportunities of full faculty professional life.[8] Just as is true with paralegals and medical paraprofessionals, that status is rarely a stepping stone to full professional licensure; it is a career path of its own.

The more innovative forms of higher education, the competency-based learning and self-paced modular "badges," further de-bundle services. At College for America (at Southern New Hampshire Uni-versity, an e-learning pioneer), a "learning coach" is assigned to each student to review students' overall progress and provide a lim-ited amount of coaching. At the end of each self-paced module, an "academic reviewer" assesses the homework or test, guaranteeing a forty-eight-hour turnaround.[9] Competency-based colleges offer accredited degrees for a fraction of the cost of traditional colleges; they do it on the backs of their parafaculty, through faster pace, lower stipends, atomized work, less latitude, and no job security.

4. **Outsourced non-core functions.** Bookstores, food service, and merchandising are increasingly conducted offsite by companies who provide equivalent services for dozens or hundreds of other organizations. Financial functions like bookkeeping and payroll, technical functions like email and web maintenance, and all kinds of easily replicable services can be hired out at a lower cost than that of keeping one's own staff. This has been a significant driver of the downsizing of the nonprofessional support staff in higher education. As a single example, Sodexo USA bills itself as the leader in "quality of life services," providing client colleges with a vast menu of possible services. Its employees will mow the lawns and trim the shrubs; they'll scrub the toilets and repair the roofs; they'll sell the tickets and the popcorn at hockey games; they'll feed the students and organize the conferences. They do these things at a competitive price by displacing individual colleges' employees with relatively lower-paid and lower-benefit workers not affiliated with the schools.

   One quiet form of cross-generation benefit that's going away due to this outsourcing is the family tuition waiver, which allows the son or daughter of the custodian to have free tuition at mom's school. For the custodian who works for Sodexo USA, Aramark, Core Management Services, or another contracted labor pool—or the contingent teacher—the college bears no family responsibility, and that step up for the next generation is lost.

5. **Replacement of humans and space with technology.** Teachers and classrooms are costly; libraries and librarians are costly; bandwidth and memory space is cheap. Colleges have responded by emphasizing online education, self-paced tutorials, lecture repositories, and study guides; and by increasing online journals, searchable whole-text databases, and electronic book leasing. All these things increase speed and convenience for the consumer while minimizing the need for human producers in physical facilities. Just as Amazon .com has been disastrous for the "brick and mortar" retail world, so the online presences in higher education, from Blackboard to JStor to Google Scholar, are placing enormous pressures on the human workers they replace.

It's uncomfortable to recognize that our consumer benefits come at the cost of worker abuse. I remember having a conversation in which my interlocutor traveled, within five minutes, from "Nothin' gets made in the US anymore, all our jobs are in China" to "I need to stop at Walmart and pick up a new barbecue grill; they're on sale"—without any intervening analysis to connect those two phenomena. And they *are* connected. Our app-driven, low-cost, vast-variety convenience is only emotionally comfortable because we don't want to take up room in our heads for jobs without benefits, jobs that aren't jobs at all. So too with higher education, all of those jobs that aren't jobs at all.[10]

This abandonment of labor has to be understood as a *necessary* condition of our desire for the ideal customer experience. Let's take cars, for instance. Here's a list of standard contemporary features that were not only uncommon but mostly unavailable at any cost on the "golden age" cars of my youth, the Mustangs, Camaros, and Barracudas that still put a shine in boomer-boys' eyes:

- performance features: fuel injection, five-speed or six-speed (or more) transmissions, radial tires, disc brakes, dual camshafts, aerodynamically optimized body shapes
- safety features: airbags, child-seat harnesses, automatic tensioning seatbelts, crumple-zone protections, safety glass, antilock brakes, traction control
- convenience features: navigation, Bluetooth, satellite radio, USB outlets, keyless entry, power plug-ins, reconfigurable seating, ubiquitous cupholders and cubbies.

All this has made the contemporary automobile faster, more fuel-efficient, safer, longer-lasting, and a greater pleasure to drive than anything available in my childhood, at a price not much different than the inflation-adjusted cost of a 1967 Ford Fairlane.

These advantages have come about not merely because of technological change, but also because the contemporary car is made under radically different labor conditions. In 1934 the Industrial Workers of the World published a document called "Unemployment and the Machine," which includes the following statement:

> In 1909 it required 303 man-hours to make one car; in 1929 the time had been reduced to 92 man-hours and in 1932 and 1933 the time is still less.[11]

According to Toyota, that's now down to below 20 hours.[12] CAD/CAM design, robotic assembly, the purchase of preassembled components, just-in-time parts provision—all of that adds up to fewer hands on the car while it runs down the assembly line at Ford's Dearborn Truck, or Honda Manufacturing of Alabama.

But there are still a lot of person-hours in a car, mostly accumulated offsite, by engineers, process managers, and components vendors. American Honda Motor Company claims on its website that it has 644 original equipment manufacturers, making everything from mirrors to motor mounts, and another 1,183 service parts suppliers to make the more generic replaceables like brake pads and batteries.[13] That's nearly two thousand businesses that don't fall under the union contracts negotiated between the major manufacturers and the UAW, never have their hands on a car under construction, never get to see it roll away from the line.

The provision of higher education has always been labor-intensive, and it continues to be so. But now much of that labor is outsourced to contingent subcontractors, classroom instructors whose engagement with the larger curriculum is nonexistent. Another large component of it resides in the hands of professional staff, working behind the scenes to organize student support systems and programs rather than engage in direct educational student contact. None of this huge, invisible community is protected under the tenure protections negotiated between the faculty and the college.

We'll always need labor. But we may not need as much of it, may not need to employ it directly, and may not need to pay as much for it.

HOPE LABOR AND THE ECONOMIES
OF THE CONTENT PROVIDER

The financial model of Web 2.0 businesses is largely the capitalization of unpaid contributions, Marx's "surplus value of labor" carried to its ultimate extremes. From YouTube to Wikipedia, from Instagram to Pinterest, from the Huffington Post to Daily Kos, the web economy is dependent on "content providers" who upload free material. And while not every poem, photograph, or funny cat video is created with one eye toward compensation, a great number of content providers do their work in the hopes of being discovered, of being plucked from the great pool of comedians, essayists, or rappers and rewarded for their labor. Communications researchers Kathleen Kuehn and Thomas Corrigan have called this phenomenon *hope labor*, which they define as "un- or under-compensated work carried out in the present, often for experience or exposure, in the hope that future employment opportunities may follow."[14]

Just as the state lottery boards and casinos publicize their handful of winners in an effort to keep the dupes at the table, so too we're beguiled with the occasional stories of someone who climbed to fame on the back of free-upload origins. A cute middle-school kid, singing on the steps at age thirteen, became Justin Bieber, with a 2017 income of $80 million at age twenty-four.[15] Snowqueen's Icedragon (?!?), writing shabby, secondhand fan-porn based on somebody else's characters in somebody else's stories, became E. L. James, making more than a hundred million dollars for books about which Salman Rushdie says, "I've never read anything so badly written that got published."[16] A flat-faced cat named Tardar Sauce appeared in a photo on Reddit and became Grumpy Cat, the pouting icon of a million-dollar marketing company.[17] The successes are notable enough that we can't say, "It'll never happen," though it happens rarely enough that we'd rightly be dubious if our son-in-law claimed it as a career strategy.

The same is true of the hope labor invested by adjunct faculty in the conviction that their excellent teaching will one day get them a seat at the big kids' table.[18] Conversion of an adjunct faculty position into a fully absorbed tenure-track career is mathematically so unlikely as to be meaningless, just like fan fiction becoming a bestseller. It *does* happen, once in a rare while, that an adjunct position might be converted into a full-time NTT job, which offers the hope at least some degree of certainty, if not legitimacy. My old postdoc group at Duke University, for instance, has four people who have been kept on as "professors of the practice," one of the many terms for the full-time NTT, even as dozens and dozens of others have cycled through the adjacent offices and into mixed futures in the past twenty years.

It's those handful that act as the shills, keeping the rest of us at the table, betting against ridiculous odds. Hope labor has become a recommended social norm. The Internet's dark masters say, "We have millions of viewers a month; think of the exposure. . . . It's a foot in the door."[19] You get your foot slammed in enough doors, you'll never walk right again. And as Dewayne Matthews of the Lumina Foundation recently wrote, in a gig economy, the stairs start at the second floor anyway.[20]

SIDE HUSTLE

> My husband is a middle-school history teacher and while he does fairly well, my teaching has definitely helped us make ends meet. Especially with the arrival of the kids . . . preschool costs $6,000+ a year per child, so basically my teaching allowed us to send both our boys to preschool. More importantly, it has allowed me to survive the up and down of having my own firm!
> —Eleanor, adjunct teacher and architect

In its examination of "the gig economy," the McKinsey Global Institute, a private think tank, developed a simple but useful matrix of independent workers, which they believe accounts for more than 150 million people in the United States and the European Union, roughly a quarter of all employment.[21] The independent workforce,

TABLE 6 The four groups of independent workers

	Primary income	Supplemental income
Preferred choice	Free agents 30%	Casual earners 40%
Out of necessity	Reluctants 14%	Financially strapped 16%

they claim, can be divided along two dimensions. The first dimension is whether freelance work constitutes their primary income, or is used to augment other income; the second is whether freelance status is a preferred or a necessary decision. The resulting matrix is seen in table 6. Now, it's not surprising that a business consulting firm would somehow discover that 70 percent of people involved in freelance work were choosing to do so, that the happy shiny world of Lyft driving, dog walking, and freelance website design just allows more scheduling latitude to meet your friends for a sixteen-dollar kale-infused bespoke cocktail and share stories of the guy you swiped right on last night in Tinder.

But, the numbers aside, the four categories help us to understand some of the confusion over "adjunct faculty." The union organizers and adjunct advocacy groups focus on the "reluctants"—the teacher who wants and is fully qualified for a regular faculty career but has not attained it and likely never will, who scrapes together a living teaching a course here and two courses there with no security and no benefits.

The higher-education community at large points to a different quadrant, the "casual earners." They love to talk about the retired professor who still comes back to teach a favorite course, the attorney who teaches one section of contract law every spring semester, the writer teaching poetry whose family is supported by a partner's salary and benefits . . . people who just can't resist teaching once in a while *because it's just so darn much fun! People who feel compelled to give back! The active professionals who give our students real-world experience*!

These casual earners in the adjunct world allow institutions to talk about contingency as a personal and social benefit, claiming that they're offering both teacher and student an opportunity that might not otherwise exist. Those stories aren't wrong. They're also not inclusive.

There's also a third quadrant represented, the financially strapped, the people who pick up a class to make up for insufficient or uncertain pay in their other professional lives. Sometimes those are already employees of the college, like the baseball coach who makes a few extra dollars teaching a strength and conditioning course. Some of them, like Eleanor, use teaching as a means of leveling an uneven professional life, or of funding contemporary essentials, like child care, that don't fit even within the budget of two adult salaries.

WOMEN'S WORK

In my two years at Michigan Tech back in the late 1970s, I took one course taught by a female professor. One, out of twenty.

When I went back to college at Berkeley in the late 1980s, I took four courses from three female professors, four courses out of twenty more. Two of the three women were adjunct.

In graduate school in Milwaukee in the early 1990s, the proportion was a little better. I took eighteen courses with eleven different professors: three of those people, accounting for seven courses, were women, and all were TT faculty.

The professoriate has long been a bastion of male expertise, of the wise expert standing distant from his flock. But this model is starting to break down, both by gender and by role. The work of the faculty is now configured much more in terms of support, "the guide on the side" replacing "the sage on the stage." And as technically focused labor (specialized expertise) is more highly paid and more highly rewarded than socially focused labor (communicative coordination), so too we see the highly paid, highly respected male professors, who proclaim from podiums, supplanted by lower-paid, less respected female faculty who do more of the hands-on work of student support.[22]

The National Center for Education Statistics shows that the fall

TABLE 7   Academic rank, by gender

	Rank	Male	Female
Tenure track	Full professor (15+ years of service)	69%	31%
	Associate professor (6–15 years of service)	56%	44%
	Assistant professor (0–6 years of service)	48%	52%
Non–tenure track	Instructors	42%	58%
	Lecturers	44%	56%

Source: National Center for Education Statistics, "Race/Ethnicity of College Faculty"

2013 cohort of full professors is 69 percent male; associate professors, 56 percent male; and assistant professors, 48 percent male (see table 7). This is evidence of increased gender equity in hiring in recent years, as well as an increased number of PhDs being awarded to women. But we also see a majority-female NTT population. This openness of the profession to women, and the shifting model of faculty life to be more service-oriented, has come at the same time as the profession has become more tenuous, more contingent, and more de-bundled. Coincidence? Not according to a significant body of economic sociology. For instance, Hadas Mandel's research describes what she calls the "up the down staircase" phenomenon of "declining discrimination against women as individual workers, and rising discrimination against occupations after the entry of women."[23] Josipa Roska's research shows college grads entering male-dominated fields at starting salaries far greater than those of college grads entering female-dominated fields.[24] Anne Lincoln's research into the "feminization" of veterinary practice demonstrates the ways in which male students begin to avoid academic disciplines that become the site of increasing women's participation.[25] Levanon, England, and Allison's research shows more evidentiary support for devaluation of "feminized professions" than for exclusion of women from "masculine professions."[26]

We see this devaluation in one industry after another. As women have entered medicine, the individual judgment of physicians has been subsumed within greater oversight and standardization of practice, and a diverse array of predominantly female paraprofessionals have come into being. As women have entered law, para-legals have emerged: two-thirds of attorneys are male, while 85 percent or more of paralegals are female.[27] And as women have entered the professoriate, we have diminished the standing and security and the unified role of the faculty.[28] I'd also propose examining the connection between the increasingly female-centric college population (the undergraduate community was 56 percent female in fall 2017) and trends of declining state funding for public higher education.[29] Regardless of the industry, the unspoken argument is the same: If a woman can do it, it must not be very important, and we shouldn't have to pay much for it.

THE TECHNOLOGICAL AVALANCHE

As in all aspects of consumer culture, higher ed is enamored of the latest technology, and quickly imagines it to be indispensable once it exists. I recently visited a college nursing program that has an entire suite fitted out as a hospital ward, with the standard array of oxygen and electrical and data infrastructure provided to each bed, the standard array of bedside intravenous pumps, blood-pressure cuffs, and heart monitors. In every bed was a medical mannequin, more than a few of which were computer-controlled and responsive to student actions. Nursing students could be presented with breathing complications, convulsions, or seizures; they could inadvertently create those conditions themselves by incorrectly administering medications. They could assist with a vaginal or a cesarean-section birth, could listen to the mannequins give self-reports of their presenting conditions to aid in diagnosis.

In an adjacent set of rooms, control centers had been set up for the observation of students by a nursing instructor. The instructor could see and hear everything in the simulation studio, could videotape the events, and could have a record of the mannequin's simulated body functions during the students' intervention. All of this could be used both to assess students in the moment, and to review performance alongside students later on.

As much as I'm in favor of nursing students injuring mannequins instead of me while they practice, it's important to recognize what an investment that simulation suite represents. And then to multiply that investment across dozens of campus locations: the computer-imagery rendering studios of the graphic design and film departments, the big-data analytics systems in marketing and geographic information systems programs, the supercomputer employed by scientists and engineers, the giant databases in use in the digital humanities. Every department on campus is a computer science department.

Individual faculty, and groups of faculty, also have research equipment of remarkable sophistication. The science departments have increasing arrays of spectrophotometers and ultracentrifuges, microfurnaces and cryofreezers, ultraviolet transilluminators and phosporimagers—tools of science once reserved only for elite researchers, but now increasingly made available to students as well. Even the model shops of architecture schools have become "fabrication labs," with 3D printers, computer-guided routers, laser cutters, and robotic-arm milling machines.

This array represents another unspoken conflict between safely tenured faculty, who get to advocate for the teaching and research tools they want, and the NTTs who are marginalized at least in part because of the cost of the TT's toolkit, and who themselves never get access to the best parts of it. So let's be blunt: Would faculty and students be better served with more tools, or with more colleagues? Who would benefit differently from different balances of those variables?

Then add on all of the nonacademic computing. The thousands of desktop computers and printers, the classrooms with their multiple LED projectors, instructor kiosks, and smartboards. The wireless network covering every building and the entire grounds besides. The email server. The faculty and staff smartphones. The learning management system, facilitating the global university archive of every course handout, every reading, every out-of-class conversation, every quiz taken, every homework submitted, every midterm and final grade, every instructor evaluation. The sweep cards that control building, room, and parking lot entry, and also record today's lunch purchase against one's prepaid meal plan. The academic records-management system coordinating financial aid, advising, registration, and transcripts for hundreds of thousands of a college's current and former students.

It's easy, in the face of this technological avalanche, to be curmudgeonly, to talk about how simple things were when one was a kid, to remind everyone how millions of people got trained to be pretty effective nurses before simulation labs. And I don't want to go there. I recognize the power of all of this technology, and I also recognize that students are being prepared to enter adult life in technologically mediated careers. All true, all important. But there are industry estimates that the annual worldwide expenditures on educational technology are approaching a quarter of a trillion dollars a year,[30] and dollars spent on technology are dollars not spent on faculty. If we're going to make the choice, we need to know that we're making the choice.

MARKETING IN A COMPETITIVE INDUSTRY

All of this technology has at least three uses. It makes lives more convenient. It makes scholarship more effective. And it acts as a powerful recruitment tool for students shopping around for both undergraduate and graduate colleges.

Just as our economy seems to be increasingly about "eyeballs," "likes," "recs," and "retweets," almost everything a college does in our current environment is linked in some way to student recruiting, to getting more casual browsers to choose a particular school from a bewildering array. The combination of reduced state funding and the post-2010 drop in high school graduates has left many schools scrambling to attract students, creating a more competitive environment in which schools constantly work to poach one another's recruitment pool.

"We're adding sports and we built a big, beautiful field house. . . . There are students who would come here if they thought there would be a real college experience. We're trying to entice those students who maybe would be attracted to a four-year institution to come here first, and for parents the draw is financial. We're saying you can save a lot of money coming to a community college for two years."

St. Clair already offered athletics programs in men's and women's basketball, baseball, softball, volleyball and golf. But last year college officials added men's and women's cross country, and this fall men's and women's bowling and wrestling will be added to the list, said Pete Lacey, St. Clair's vice president of student services. Tennis and women's soccer are under consideration for the future.

Lacey said the college's administrators are budget conscious and recognize their sports programs aren't lucrative, but they're optimistic the additional enrollment will offset any increases in cost.

— Smith and Lederman, "Enrollment Declines,
    Transfer Barriers"[31]

If a college is going to effectively sell enrollment space on an increasingly open market, it has to differentiate itself from its competition. At the same time, colleges need to respond to the pressures of standardization: disciplinary and institutional accreditation, transfer credits, the commodification of the bachelor's degree. So, if they can't differentiate their academic experience, they need something else, and that something else often consists of easily photographed and tour-friendly amenities such as student centers, science buildings, athletic opportunities, and technological bling. They expand sports programs to attract male students, now that working-class and middle-class undergraduate education has become a primarily female endeavor.[32] Even a community college—St. Clair County Community College in post-industrial eastern Michigan—has built a giant fieldhouse, as much for its shock-and-awe value in recruitment as for any improvement in the lived experience of students. It's an advertisement in the form of a building, every bit as much a branding exercise as hiding the dull history of a name like St. Clair County Community College behind the high-tech image of the "SC4" logo.

THE PIG IN THE SNAKE

One last large cultural force I'll mention is the lasting impact of the baby boom, which has caused massive fluctuation in age-related social expenses from its birth through its retirement, simply because of its sheer size compared to adjacent generational cohorts. Table 8 shows the impact of US births on colleges, in both undergraduate student demand and faculty demand.

Even if the percentage of high school graduates going to college had remained stable over those years, these kinds of demographic shifts would place enormous demands on colleges. Couple that with the increased college-going rate, though, and it's easy to see why colleges experienced massive booms in enrollment, construction, and new programs in the decade of the 2000s, with numbers of eighteen-year-olds not seen since the 1960s and '70s. And the recent trend of births has been relatively flat since 1995. The college population we have now in 2017 is about what we're going to have for the next twenty years, which is part of why so many schools are adding master's programs—they need to make their enrollment numbers, and

TABLE 8   US births per year, and arrival at college-relevant milestones

Birth year	Number of births	Change in five years	Year at age 18 (new freshman)	Year at age 30 (new faculty)	Year at age 70 (retirement)
1945	2,735,000	—	1963	1975	2015
1950	3,554,000	+30%	1968	1980	2020
1955	4,104,000	+15%	1973	1985	2025
1960	4,258,000	+4%	1978	1990	2030
1965	3,760,000	−12%	1983	1995	2035
1970	3,731,000	±0%	1988	2000	2040
1975	3,144,000	−16%	1993	2005	2045
1980	3,612,000	+15%	1998	2010	2050
1985	3,761,000	+4%	2003	2015	2055
1990	4,158,000	+11%	2008	2020	2060
1995	3,900,000	−6%	2013	2025	2065
2000	4,059,000	+4%	2018	2030	2070
2005	4,138,000	+2%	2023	2035	2075
2010	3,999,000	−3%	2028	2040	2080
2015	3,978,000	−1%	2033	2045	2085

Source: National Center for Health Statistics, "Vital Statistics of the United States"

adding grad students is a way to do that in the face of level or falling undergrad recruits.

Let's look at the boomers, the first massive pig in the snake. Births throughout the 1950s and into 1960 were at record highs, which meant that the boomers went to college between 1965 and 1980. They became parents in the 1980s and early '90s, providing colleges with a 2000s echo boom. Those who went into faculty life did so at about that same time, in the '80s and '90s.

But a funny thing happened to the hippies, the college kids of the 1960s who became the faculty of the 1980s and the college leaders of the 1990s and 2000s. First of all, torn jeans and sandals aside, they represented an economically and culturally comfortable group of students, representing the 40 percent threshold of high school-to-college rather than the contemporary 70 percent, still mostly white and disproportionately male (especially with Vietnam draft defer-ments still possible for college boys). For the most part, the faculty were recruited from research universities that had already winnowed the working class out of participation, resulting in an even more rari-fied community. As that group took over the operation of colleges in the 1980s and '90s, they remained cultural elites, connected to the savvy political climate of the Reagan '80s and the "third way" '90s, increasingly seduced by the progress and consumerism they had once questioned. Now in their sixties, they'll never retire (the average age of college faculty retirement is now over seventy-two), their retirement accounts are looking good, and they've raised the drawbridges behind them.[33]

Prior generations created a wealth of legacy resources; the boom-ers demanded more, used them up, and never replaced them when they were done. Interstate highways and subway systems . . . cheap gas and cheap electricity . . . unions . . . safe careers . . . all things pro-vided by the workers of the first half of the century to the boomers, and left to be scarce, failing or unavailable to those under fifty.

Look again at table 7, at the column showing the period during which birth cohorts reached prospective faculty age. The boomer cohort was entering the faculty in the late 1970s through 1990, just as colleges were ramping up to meet the echo boom; real academic jobs were more widely available in that window. But the big cohort of 1990s and 2000s college kids they served, at least the ones who went on to grad school, are now entering an academic job market that has no more interest in expansion.

In almost every arena of life, we've seen how the boomer demographic temporarily inflated the stock of some enterprises, only to leave them at the curb when the excitement died down and the next phase of collective life span appeared. From marijuana to cocaine to Viagra, from investment in education to tax revolts, from the Mustang to the minivan to the Miata, from birthing suites to long-term residential care, the market's attention has repeatedly reflected sheer cohort numbers. And as the boomers' careers are winding down, secure faculty employment . . . secure *any* employment . . . is one of those discards.

CONTINGENCY AS THE SUM OF ALL TRENDS

A few years back, there was a lot of talk about "peak oil," the moment at which petroleum production had reached its highest rate and begun to decline. This peak and decline has spurred a post-oil paradigm of renewable energy, a flurry of creative responses to energy needs without the belief in a limitless supply of fossil fuels. It's also spurred a desperate last-ditch effort to frack our way into new supplies. Adaptations to new circumstances aren't always smart.

I think we have likewise passed the point of peak faculty. A combination of consumer thinking, market fluidity, loss of professional status, technological innovation, and demographic shifts has led us to a point where the faculty will never again be a primarily full-time, primarily tenure-track institutional or cultural commitment. There will always be teachers, sure. But the idea of "the faculty" is as dead as the idea of coal; it'll carry on for a while because of sunk costs and the gasping demands of those still left in the industry—but really, it's gone.

What will replace it is yet to be discovered. We are in a time of great disruption, and a lot of people won't make it through.

8

WHAT TO DO?

The preceding chapters have laid out the diagnosis of contingency. But diagnosis is incomplete without prescription and intervention. What should we do, from our own positions as students or parents or teachers?

Let me tell you a story.

THE PARABLE OF THE FISHES

On June 15 [1967], while on a flight to investigate sources of pollution in Lake Michigan, an official of the Great Lakes Region of the Federal Water Pollution Control Administration spotted long white streaks in the water. The Navy Hydroplane in which he was riding dipped lower. The streaks were windrows of dead alewives, belly-up. The wind was blowing the dead and dying fish toward the Michigan side of the lake. The official observed one great shimmering band of alewives stretching for 40 miles between Muskegon and South Haven, Michigan. On June 17, an article in the *Chicago Sun-Times* mentioned the dead fish and how they had become an annual pollution problem by littering beaches and producing a noxious stench. Over the weekend, June 17–18, however, the wind shifted, blowing from east to west. By Monday, June 19, Chicago's 30 miles

of shoreline was clogged with a silvery carpet of alewive carcasses
... the great alewife invasion of 1967 was on. . . .
—Federal Water Pollution Control Administration, 1967 [1]

I grew up in Muskegon Heights, Michigan, and I was nine years old
during this event, a summer die-off that resulted in an estimated
twenty billion dead alewives washed ashore on the beaches of the
entire southern basin of Lake Michigan, from Milwaukee to Muskegon. I remember the beach at Pere Marquette Park, swarming with
flies. Fish bulldozed into mountains, gleaming pyramids of dead alewives decomposing in the summer sun.

The alewife is a herring that travels upriver to spawn in fresh water
before returning to the oceans. For millennia, the alewife was concentrated along the Atlantic coast of North America, up the rivers
from Boston, Newport, St. John, New York, and then back into
deep water. But when the Erie Canal was cut across upstate New
York from the Hudson River, the alewife followed the canal. Lakes
Ontario and Erie had a permanent alewife population by the earliest
part of the twentieth century, followed by Lake Huron in 1933, Lake
Michigan in 1949, and Lake Superior in 1954.[2]

On its own, the arrival of the alewives would not have been a terrible thing. Lake trout think alewives are tasty; people think lake
trout are tasty. But people thought trout were so tasty, and so fun
to catch, that they were grossly overfished in the 1930s and beyond,
once more boats had internal combustion engines and could thus
operate further offshore for longer amounts of time under a wider
variety of conditions. Fewer trout, more alewives. And there's your
smoking gun: murder by modern fishing boat.

But no. The lake trout were taken down by fishermen, absolutely.
But their numbers were already decimated. The population explosion of the alewife crowded out a lot of other small fish, creating a
vitamin imbalance in the predatory trout that weakened their ability
to reproduce. And, paradoxically, alewives themselves eat a lot of
trout eggs and larvae, thus reducing the numbers of trout that mature

into predation of their own. Then the knockout blow: the introduction of another ocean creature, the sea lamprey. Lamprey are foul beasts, basically oversized leeches that gnaw onto any animal they can get hold of (including people who dare to swim in their waters), dissolving its muscle tissue and blood into a kind of smoothie. Like the alewives, the lampreys migrated from the Atlantic into the Great Lakes, mostly by being sucked up into the ballast holds of empty ships coming to the industrial ports of Cleveland, Detroit, Milwaukee, and Chicago and the iron mines of Wisconsin and Minnesota, where that water was discharged and its weight displaced by cars, steel, and taconite pellets. As Midwestern industrialization thrived, the lamprey spread, and the trout population was devastated before the fishermen ever had a chance. Commercial trout harvest in Lake Michigan dropped from three million kilograms in 1944 to near zero by 1951.[3] And the alewives, in the absence of their primary predator, bred and bred and bred.

All those dead fish on the shore of my beach in 1967 had their origins a hundred forty years earlier in the Erie Canal, which was developed to bring Midwestern grain to East Coast ports. They had their origins in the World War II industrial effort and the postwar boom, in every Buick sedan and every Allis Chalmers tractor, every Iowa ham and every case of Sherwin Williams paint loaded onto an oceanbound freighter. Twenty billion dead alewives was not a crime scene; it was the ecological outcome of millions and millions of decisions, each innocuous on its own, but collectively resulting in an unparalleled instability that no one had ever imagined.

In the subsequent decades we could have left the lake alone. We could have thrown up our hands once we discovered how systemic the issues were, and claimed that the problem was beyond us. We could have decided that as lamentable as it all was, we wouldn't want to inconvenience any of the industries that relied on the status quo.

Fortunately for all of us, the response was something other than that. The states bordering Lake Michigan agreed to import Pacific Chinook and Coho salmon as predators to replace the lake trout.

Increased controls over industrial and agricultural runoff stabilized the algaes and plankton that fed the smaller fish. Regulations were passed to prohibit the indiscriminate sale of fishing bait, which often had become disruptive after escape and reproduction. Boatwashing stations and lake quarantines reduced the spread of zebra and quagga mussels. The lamprey population was knocked back through the use of larvicides, physical barriers, traps, and ballast-water exchange protocols. And scholars worked to better understand the ways in which the Great Lakes were influenced by their connections with hundreds of thousands of glacial lakes, rivers, and marshlands. All of the factories, farmers, and fishermen of the Great Lakes changed their practices—some eagerly, some grudgingly, some looking for ways to quietly not comply. And the massive die-offs have stopped.

THE SHATTERED ECOSYSTEM OF HIGHER EDUCATION

Fifty years on, we see a million or more gasping adjuncts and post-docs washed up on the beaches of academia, piled up in heaps at community colleges and regional state schools, crowded into writing programs and remedial courses, bulldozed aside from the intellectual lives they hoped to join, starving as they do the heavy lifting of higher ed so that their TT superiors needn't dirty their hands.

This die-off is likewise the result of innumerable decisions, each reasonable on its own but resulting in a species in crisis. We produce far too many new scholars and use far too few. Changes taking place within higher education—fluctuating enrollments of students chasing unpredictable careers, the reduction of public funding, the ubiquity of transfer students, the rise of the co-curricular college professionals, increased regulatory and disciplinary demands for standardization—work against stable academic careers. Changes in our larger culture—the privilege of consumption over production, the normalization of "hope labor," the devaluation of every profession that women gain access to, the unreflective embrace of progress, the primacy of marketing and the ritual of expansion, and the lasting impacts of the baby boom—have made the disaster of faculty unemployment seem normal. And our lack of agreed understanding about why college exists at all, and for whom, presents a convoluted problem perhaps too tangled to straighten out.

We didn't arrive at our mass beaching of the adjuncts in a couple of misguided years, and we're not going to get away from it with a handful of key actions, whether it be a push to unionization, the opening of another thousand colleges, another political statement on the conditions of part-time faculty, or a new job app with which departments and adjuncts can look at one another's profiles and swipe right on our favorites. We are dealing with a systemic crisis, the equivalent of a species die-off, and we must think systemically about our responses.

NAMING OUR DREAMS, NOT JUST OUR FEARS

It's emotionally challenging. There's just a lot of unknowns. I try not to get frustrated. I like my students, I enjoy the teaching I'm doing, but I don't have a TA, and I have a hundred students across the three classes, so that's frustrating. I'm also teaching one course at [nearby state school], about forty minutes away. Both schools have had budget cuts, so there's not likely to be any work here this fall. And it's draining to apply and not get jobs, after having done so much work.
—Marianne, first-year NTT

When I teach writing, I tell my students that they can never know who their audience is. What you *can* do, I tell them, is to decide for yourself what you want to be true about the world because your book or article exists, and then imagine who your allies might be if you could persuade them to take up the cause.

That question has haunted me during the entirety of this project. What exactly *is* it that I want to be true about the world, or at least the world of higher education? And who can help?

I want every student to have the opportunity to become someone different from what she thinks she is. I want every student to change majors in light of discovering a new love, a new way of thinking about the world that's greater than the one she thought she wanted. I want every student at every level to have two or three teachers she's comfortable getting lunch or coffee with, people she'll see regularly for a couple of years instead of once or twice a week for a semester.

I want every young grad student to understand why she's a scholar, what she herself wants to be true about the world because of her work. I want her to be a teaching assistant not just at her own university, but at three or four different kinds of schools, so that she learns something about the array of higher ed and its students, learns what forms of service are most compelling. And I want scholarly ways of thinking—not content mastery, but the desire to constantly break a problem open, to question why it matters, to keep in mind who benefits and who is set aside—to lead to multiple career opportunities, rather than being sequestered only within the academy.

I want every faculty member to know that her core function, regardless of content knowledge, is relationship facilitation. I want every faculty member to be an evangelist for her way of knowing the world, and to welcome the excited, hesitant initiates with coffee and love and a network of new colleagues. I want her to make calls on behalf of her grad students, take her young charges out for drinks at the national conference to meet the smartest, most powerful people she knows at other schools, and build bonds among them.

I want every faculty member to know that along with offering membership in a new culture and a new community, she's also reshaping an existing membership with her student's family and friends. As students change, as they grow in unpredictable ways; they will become familiar aliens to the people who loved them as they were. I want that faculty member to help her students understand their coming lives as dual citizens, and I want colleges to work with family members to help them support their children's growth into adults still beloved even if only partly recognizable.

I want every faculty hiring committee to look closely at the people around them, the student teachers and the contingent faculty who work diligently with their students. I want the existing faculty and their chairs and deans to find the smart and good-hearted people among them and give them more to do, more chances to grow into the work, and then reward them for their success, just as would be done at any other workplace in America. I want them to forego the national search for the possible star, and instead reward local favorites who've already proven themselves capable in their specific context.

And unicorns. Did I mention the unicorns?

We're so entrenched in our current ways of doing things that all these desires seem childishly utopian. The realists among us will say, "Oh, we could *never* do that," or "That would *never* work," and then turn, knowing grownups that they are, back to the management of the everyday tragedy of everyday practices.

But let's be clear. What we're doing now doesn't work. It doesn't work for a million or more teachers, and doesn't work for the half of students who start college and don't finish. It doesn't even work for the people securely inside higher ed, working 24/7 at the expense of their families and personal lives. Let's not pretend that any changes would be a risky departure from successful operations, asking us to surrender some nearly ideal current state.

Let's also be clear that there are no "good old days" that we want to get back to, that we'd be fine if only we could turn back the calendar to the 1970s, or the 1870s, or Plato and the School of Athens. There is no argument for originalism in higher education. We don't want to return to the nineteenth century, when any half-baked denomination or real estate huckster could start a "college" without meaningful guidance or oversight. We don't want to return to the 1930s, when the sons of the elite filled most college seats, when fewer than 10 percent of our kids went to college and the majority of Americans hadn't finished high school. We don't want to return to the 1950s, when so many colleges were racially segregated by policy, and most campus organizations were racially segregated in fact of daily life. We don't want to return to the 1970s, when the fact of women at so many colleges was still so unusual that we casually employed the term "coeds." We don't want to return to the 1990s, when tiny rainbow triangles were snuck onto the doors of a few faculty offices, marking them as rare spots of safety where a student—or a colleague—could be open about gender and sexual identity.

Wishing for the colleges of thirty or fifty or a hundred years ago is like wishing for the cars of thirty or fifty or a hundred years ago. We now have colleges that are richer, stronger, more inclusive, and more effective than those of our forebears. We got to this place through the collective result of millions of intelligent decisions, millions of individuals acting in good will toward good ends. We have built a model of higher ed that serves a greater proportion of our population, that leads the world in scientific sophistication. American higher education is increasingly capable of working with students from a broad array of ethnic, cultural, gender, sexual, and political identities; a broad array of physical and intellectual abilities; a broad array of economic and class backgrounds.

Nobody made a direct, ruthless policy decision to use contingent faculty and postdocs as the expendable species in this shifting system. Nobody decided that having unemployed scholars was a good thing. The die-off just came with the territory while we weren't paying attention; we didn't see them until they were beached in massive numbers. Changing that ecosystem will not be painless; it will cause us to modify other good things, and to question our core values in the process.

RECOMMENDATIONS FOR SURVIVAL
IN THE CURRENT CLIMATE

My first recommendations are in the spirit of Red Cross triage: they're imperfect and messy, but we're trying to save some lives in the midst of a disaster.

For prospective undergraduate students and their families:

1. If you go to community college or to a middle-class school, know that you'll be relying heavily, at least for the first couple of years, on people who aren't your teachers. Advising and counseling services and the office of undergraduate research will be there on an everyday basis, whereas the person in front of you in the classroom may not. Make sure you know about and take full advantage of the people at the school who are paid to be with you steadily on this journey, because your teachers won't be.

2. Ask each one of your teachers what their status is. Are they part-time, full-time on contract, or tenure-track? At the end of each semester, advocate for your best teachers, not just on course evaluations and RateMyProfessor.com, but through writing letters to the deans who oversee their departments. And get those teachers' personal email addresses — you might have questions down the road for which you trust their judgment, and they're used to working for free anyway.

3. Commit to your education in every way possible, even at the expense of other things that seem like necessities. Changing your life is not a part-time endeavor. There's an old saying in architecture that you can have a building cheap, you can have it fast, or you can have it good — pick any two. College is much the same: you can have an education cheap, you can have it convenient, or you can have it good. They don't all happen together.

For prospective grad students:

4. Download a copy of the National Research Council's assessment of doctoral programs, and be cautious about applying to any school not in the top 10 percent of its discipline. Lots of doctoral programs can give you a wonderful intellectual experience; only a few of them are likely to give you a chance in the labor market.

5. Once you've settled on a school, choose the three or four faculty members you're most likely to work with there. Learn who their current and most recent dissertation students are. Talk to those

students about their experience of being mentored, or ignored, or abused. Listen closely, between the lines. Believe what you hear.

For colleges and their management:

6. Every time you're asked to buy new or upgraded technology, or to start a new academic support program, ask yourself what percentage of a faculty member it would cost. Sit quietly for a couple of hours with the question of whether these tools would benefit your students more than another strong member of your community.

7. Be honest with every contingent member of your faculty about their chances for permanence. Advertise with integrity, and don't even hint at possibilities that you know are unlikely. If you overhear one of your adjunct faculty casually talk about her hopes for staying on for the long term, call her in for a talk and let her know it won't happen—not because she's not wonderful, but because you're structured for impermanence.

8. If you have a significant research agenda, consider staffing more and more of the work with professional laboratory personnel rather than relying on an endless stream of disposable grad students. If Pfizer and Microsoft can pay their employees, so can you.

These small habits will lead all of us to operate with greater clarity, greater dignity, and some hope of success within the system as it exists today.

But let's get bigger. Let's look at some things we might do to reduce our burden of contingency, if we were brave, and why they might be powerful for everyone involved.

PRINCIPLED ACTION

Every one of these catalytic places will push and stretch you beyond what you think possible; they'll let you slip and slide and they'll help you find your footing, but they won't let you hide from your potential or yourself. . . . Teaching is an act of love. Students and professors develop a mentor relationship in class, and professors become students' hiking companions, intramural teammates, dinner hosts and friends. Learning is collaborative rather than competitive; values are central, community matters. These colleges are places of great coherence, where the whole becomes greater than the sum of its parts.

—Loren Pope[4]

About twenty years ago, *New York Times* education editor Loren Pope published a book called *Colleges That Change Lives*, an examination of colleges that took as their primary mission the development of students as whole people, not as workers or protoprofessionals or grad students in training. The forty colleges he lists (and the book has been updated four times, with some early inclusions dropping away and others coming on board) offer powerful opportunities for young people to become great.

Although he doesn't claim to be exhaustive, he did go out of his way to name specific schools and the details of why they mattered. He identified forty colleges that change lives—out of 4,700. A little less than 1 percent. What would the books be called about the others? It'd be a pretty uninspired array of titles.

> *Colleges That Get You Ready to Go to Another College*
> *Colleges That Leave You More or Less the Way You Were, But Teach*
> *   You to Be a Nurse*
> *Colleges of Infinite Choice Wrapped around a Hollow Core*
> *Colleges That Will Ensure That Your Family's Privilege Continues*
> *   Unbroken*
> *Colleges That Will Keep Your Parents' Unspoken Disappointment at*
> *   Bay for a Little While Longer*

Let's be serious. A college should take as its fundamental mission the opportunity to change the lives of everyone within it. Otherwise, it should call itself something else: a trade school, a federal research laboratory, an NBA training camp, or a young adult day care center.

Here are four guiding principles I'd like to propose for any college worthy of its station. Individual colleges could manifest these principles in innumerable ways, to fit their particular community and its values. But regardless of their specific form, these principles would help a school constantly move toward its aspirations rather than being always driven by fear, scarcity, and external codes. And they would make contingency impossible.

PRINCIPLE ONE: RELATIONSHIPS ARE EVERYTHING

We are not merely economic units, not merely student and teacher, not merely roles in a classroom, not merely vaults of knowledge or streams of data. We are all people, trying to become something greater than we are, and looking for others who can help. We are all going to die one day, and we will be remembered for the lives we've made better—not for our ability to explain the work of Arundhati Roy or Roy Lichtenstein, but for our ability to help students place themselves and ideas together in a larger context, and to help them understand why other complex, whole people have made the decisions they have.

Every person has a particular blend of knowledge and enthusiasms, of capabilities and concerns. Rather than trim some of that away as being extraneous, outside our discipline, or our body of knowledge, colleges could begin with the presumption that we are all entire, that nothing about us is extraneous. There's a remarkable body of research on the enduring power and importance of the relationships we form in college, with our friends and with our favorite teachers. They show us new ways to be our best selves, get us through dark nights of the soul, open doors to worlds unimagined. Those relationships and the character they develop, far more than an ability to calculate heat transfer through wall structures, will make our futures.

A college based on relationships would not allow for the instrumental treatment of any of its members, would not permit exploitation of teacher, student, groundskeeper, or football player. It would ask us all to begin with the presumption of good will and good intentions, and would have us all allotted a full ration of respect and dignity from first encounter onward. It would honor every moment of transition—not merely tests and graduation day, but arrivals and unexpected departures, changes of status and markers of achievement along the way. When conflicts arise, as they always do, a college based on relationships would ask who is most at risk, who has the most at stake and the fewest resources to weather the storms.[5] It would put its best teachers with its entering students, would give its most uncertain new members the strongest stairs to climb. It would remind us of our responsibility to intervene in the face of cruelty. It would lift the weak to become strong.

A college based on relationships would know that every member of the community comes with relationships already established, every student and teacher already with spouses and parents and friends. It would ask us to be kind to them as well—to not interrupt their evenings, weekends, and vacations with the nagging email tapping on their shoulders. It would ask us to acknowledge to students' family members that their relationships will change due to their child's explorations, but that the change needn't be traumatic, needn't be a rejection of the past. A college based on relationships might offer some of that growth in small ways to family members as well.

A college based on relationships would not align itself with distant standards, would not subdivide its experiences to buy or sell on the transfer market. A college based on relationships would embrace its unique work, enabled by its unique faculty and pursued by its unique students. It would reflect the physical and cultural landscape within which it lives—a college in a metropolis would be different than a college in the country, a college in the mountains different than a college on the prairie, because of the culture and the resources that form its context. It would be not generic but specific, and every person within it would change its chemistry in small but knowable ways.

PRINCIPLE TWO: THE FACULTY IS THE COLLEGE

As Niccole, our ten-year adjunct working across three different states, put it, "What else are you in university for but to take classes from professors? The majority of the tuition should go to that." What would happen if we actually acted that way?

We'd obviously increase the proportion of full-time faculty, so that students could have ongoing experiences with adults whom they'd come to trust, and so that faculty could see individual students growing over time and across areas of performance. Schools would still have a small number of part-time faculty, teaching specialized courses or covering for an unexpected family leave, but the overwhelming majority of student contact would be with a stable, enduring teacher.

We'd decrease the proportion of professional staff as well, instead letting the faculty members take over the work of counseling, advising, service learning, study abroad, undergraduate research, admissions, recreation, and intramural sports. I know that these are all areas of specialized knowledge, and not just anybody can do them well. But people with doctorates aren't just anybody. To quote a friend, a faculty member and former provost: "Having a PhD means that I've demonstrated my ability to learn a lot of things quickly and well." With a little dedicated training, a smart person can manage admissions counseling or an intramural soccer league. If a faculty member's workload went from four courses per semester down to two courses plus coordinating the school's study-abroad offerings, students would see her repeatedly *and* in different roles, and would learn something about her enthusiasms aside from sociology or electrophysics.

If we believed that the faculty was the college, we'd also have faculty manage most of its executive functions as well. We could easily imagine a president and a provost elected by the faculty, from the faculty, for a temporary term before going back to their daily roles of student contact. That's how we run most small-city governments, after all—choosing from among our neighbors to temporarily manage and budget for the plowing of roads and the provision of fire services. Only empires need emperors; colleges with humility govern themselves.

But a more radical reading of this principle might be even more exciting. We might imagine the collective noun *the faculty* to really be capable of collective action. The faculty, as a whole, might hire its new members rather than shopping the job out to its departments. The faculty, after all, would be responsible for the entirety of the school, and thus have a stake in selecting all of its new members, looking for people who could not merely teach needed topics but, more importantly, add to the culture and breadth of the school.

The faculty might also collectively determine the next generation of students. They already do this department-by-department for their doctoral students, so it's not an unfamiliar task. So let that body of faculty review the applicants, have the conversations with prospective students and family, and bring on board the kinds of students who would thrive within their school while perhaps pushing it a little further.

PRINCIPLE THREE: EVERYBODY LEARNING ALL THE TIME

The stereotypical formulation of education is that there is one person in the room who knows, and a group of others who do not yet know. This places the teacher in a paradoxically passive position, the only person without an intellectual task to accomplish.

Just under a century ago, the psychologist Lev Vygotsky coined the term *zone of proximal development* (commonly referred to as the ZPD) to mark the kinds of problems that foster learning rather than either stasis or confusion. The fundamental idea is that a teacher or parent gives a child a task that's just over their head, and then assists them in figuring out how to do it. After a short while, the child can do it on their own, and we can move the bar up just a little higher.

In a college worthy of its station, everyone involved would be in the ZPD most of the time. A college in the zone would be founded upon the habit of seeing a problem, messy and undefined and insoluble, and walking into it rather than shying away and leaving it to others. A college in the zone would ask us to say yes to new opportunities even when we're not entirely sure of our capability, and to find colleagues who could help us take them on. A college in the zone would constantly be on the lookout for new ways for all of its members to scare themselves with something bigger than what they think they can do, and would recruit its new faculty from its best part-timers and its best grad students, lifting them up to new and more thorough engagement with the community.

A college in the zone would acknowledge that students carry knowledge as well, knowledge that teachers wouldn't possess: knowledge of changing culture, of new music, of positions of identity that are unfamiliar to their older colleagues. It would build the expectation that everybody on campus is a teacher, that everybody on campus is a learner.

The members of a college in the zone would not often say, "That'll never work." They would more often say, "Let's try it and see." The members of a college in the zone would be less concerned with institutional consistency, and more concerned with possibilities that present themselves. Mistakes of exuberance would replace mistakes of missed opportunity or mistakes of self-imposed constraint.

PRINCIPLE FOUR: PROVE IT

In our fetish for quantification, we've created mythology: the belief that a total of 120 credits marks a bachelor's degree, that a grade of B+ is measurably something other than a grade of A–, that a tenured associate professor has proven her worth permanently. But in an empirical rather than mythological culture, workers would be promoted on the basis of quality work rather than time employed. Spouses would never imagine trying to calculate a B+ for their husband's past three months of parental responsibility. If readers thought that the last two books of an author we'd once loved were unsatisfying, we'd stop reading her.

An empirical rather than mythological culture would ask to see good work. We'd have constant discussions about what good work looked like, negotiations about priorities for next steps, regular feedback about everybody's satisfactions and everybody's concerns.

We've regularized things that should be unique, put proxies onto things that should be examined directly. And we've done it to ourselves. There's no law, for instance, that says that a student has to declare a major in some department. What the relevant standards say is that students must have the opportunity, and obligation, to develop an area of specific and personally chosen interest, and to demonstrate strong capability in its theories and practices, its body of knowledge and its methods of knowledge creation.[6] If we believed in that fundamental practice rather in than the number of credits and a grade point average, we'd ask for regular demonstrations of each student's status, and confer with them over the next stages of growth that would lead toward mastery. If we believed in continual intellectual growth for our faculty, we'd ask that they regularly demonstrate an effective employment of their curiosity, and confer with them over their next steps.

Any college worthy of its station would be flooded with constant performance, with planned and opportunistic demonstrations of enthusiasm brought to high standards of execution. There's be book talks by the authors and dance recitals by the choreographers. There'd be formal concerts by the college orchestra, and impromptu performances at the student union by fluid arrays of student and faculty musicians. We wouldn't wait until finals week in December or May to show what we could do; we'd be showing it all the time. From first-year students to senior faculty to dining staff, the campus would be alive with demonstrated enthusiasms.

A performance-centered college would foster regular conversations about excellence, in general and in specific. It would develop connoisseurs able to discern small differences and explain their importance. It would develop enthusiast leaders able to explain the nuances of their practices in ways that illuminate them for the lay audience.

THE SUM OF THE FOUR PRINCIPLES

Let's recap these four guiding principles into a sort of mission statement.

> A worthy college works to foster and to respect its web of relationships. It is a culture shaped and steered by its faculty. It places everyone into a place of continual learning. It asks for regular public demonstration of that learning.

These four principles would make contingency unthinkable. To show that more clearly, let's state the opposite of each principle:

> A college should privilege content knowledge over the people who carry it. It is a business shaped and steered by its managers. It places people into fixed roles of fixed expertise. It examines and measures the proxies of learning, evaluated only by an internal disciplinary audience.

This latter statement is a perfect breeding medium for contingency, and it's what we take for granted but never say about college as it exists today. It is the unspoken mission statement of almost every college and university I've ever visited.

We will not eliminate contingency through battles, through unions and collective bargaining, because we can make a school pay people better without respecting them any more fully. We will not eliminate contingency through increased state or federal funding, because we've already demonstrated that there are any number of things to spend money on that are more appealing than a permanent faculty. We will not eliminate contingency through the oversight of accreditors, because we've experienced their willingness to award continued operation to schools that starve the majority of their teachers.

We will only eliminate contingency through changing our definitions and our values. We will only eliminate it through cultivating respect, through the decision to reward demonstrated capability and good will rather than roles in an organizational chart.

It will take a brave school to engage these conversations. Most won't bother, preferring the devil they know. They will surrender without struggle, laying out for examination the hundred reasons why their hands are tied. And the weakest members of their community—students and teachers alike—will continue to bear the highest costs.

AFTERMATH

LIFE IN EXILE

My wife completed her PhD in environmental psychology in 1982, from the Graduate Center of the City University of New York, having done her dissertation on the ways in which people constructed for themselves a sense of place, of home, of lineage, in the Pine Barrens of New Jersey.

In the technology of that time, she sent a typewritten copy of her dissertation to University Microfilms International in Ann Arbor, the nation's repository of master's theses and doctoral dissertations. She bought from them a dozen or so copies of the bound dissertation, at forty or fifty dollars apiece: for herself, for her parents, for close friends, and for the members of her dissertation committee.

Months later, she received a small, handwritten note from one of those committee members. I will reproduce it here in full.

7/19

Dear Nora,

(I hope this reaches you.)

Thanks for your note and copy of thesis. I appreciate your kind words.

I hope you still believe it was all worthwhile. You worked so hard (sometimes!) and it hasn't seemed to lead anywhere.

Best,

———————

Nora subsequently taught at Rutgers, at Pratt Institute, at the New York School of Interior Design, at the Fashion Institute of Technology, at the Boston Architectural College, at Green Mountain College, and at Castleton State College. She started teaching in 1982, and taught through the 1980s, 1990s, and 2000s, up until 2014: thirty years of course-by-course contracts, of outstanding course evaluations and devoted students, of collegiality offered to deaf ears and turned shoulders.

I finished my dissertation in late 1996, to high praise and rapid publication. I went on to sell furniture. I went on to measure the illumination of prison perimeter lighting and the duration of stay of juvenile offenders. I went on to be bewildered that in my two years in a school reform organization, we talked so rarely about kids. I went on to a teaching postdoc at age forty-four, much later than most TT faculty have successfully been safely tenured. I went on to take one administrative position and then another at a professional college that had little room for broader intellectual life. I went on to hold leadership positions as a volunteer in one of the innumerable symbiont organizations of higher education, surrounded by those who had made it, who had somehow passed through the gates that had closed in the face of my pleas. I searched their successes as I considered my failure.

I lost most of my forties to what I can only refer to as a nervous breakdown. Grief will make you crazy, and I was impossible to live with, even for myself. I showed up for work, and that's about the best that can be said for me. The four years of teaching at Duke saved me, at least during the daylight hours, but I did that whole job with one eye on the calendar, knowing that my time in heaven had an expiration date, after which I'd be cast out once again.

I've tried very hard in working on this project to focus outward, to talk about what's happening around me, to find facts and make connections. But the grief of not finding a home in higher ed—of having done everything as well as I was capable of doing, and having it not pan out . . . of being told over and over how well I was doing and how much my contributions mattered, even as the prize was withheld—consumed more than a decade. It affected my physical health. It affected my mental health. It ended my first marriage. It re-opened all my fears from childhood about abandonment and rejection. It was a chasm into which I fell during the job search of 1996–97, and from which I didn't really fully emerge until I left higher ed altogether in 2013.

Over the past year I've helped two colleges with their accreditation efforts. I've put on a few faculty development events. And now I'm writing about the contingent academic workforce. And I realize how much I resent it all. I resent being the one who tries to be fair, who tries to take a balanced, holistic view of the misfortunes of hundreds of thousands of my contingent colleagues, and the safe and often un-remarkable permanent careers of hundreds of thousands of others.

Every contact I have with higher education brings me right back into the chasm. Into envious comparisons with others. Into the com-monsense conclusion that *of course* I wasn't good enough, *of course* I did something wrong along the way. Into trying to be rational, ana-lytical, and strategic about something as fundamental as my own identity as a scholar and teacher and colleague.

I went with my wife on a research trip recently in support of her current project. We were in Hennicker, New Hampshire, home of New England College. As we drove through the compact campus and its white clapboard buildings, I was immediately beguiled once again with the life I wanted: to have been the kind, wise man who led generations of students into a richer adulthood on a protected, monastic grounds. The music of a good college campus always makes me sing, and having that song inside me again even momen-tarily made me realize how much the silence has ached.

The problems with the adjunct structure of higher education are not merely quantitative. It's not just about how badly adjuncts are paid, not just about the inadequate opportunities for our students to build enduring relationships with the faculty who guide them. It's also about fear, despair, surrender, shame . . . the messy, hidden human elements that finance and policy always miss.

Writing this book has come at great cost. I have, once again, been called to be reasonable in the face of inexplicable grief, to attempt to find a place in my heart and my head for a community that could find no such place for me.

The story of the adjunct faculty, of the postdoctoral scholars, of those in "alt-careers"—that story will be incomplete unless we recognize that we are refugees from a nation that would not have us. We have found our way to innumerable continents, but still hold that lost home in our hearts. We still, many of us, in quiet moments, mourn the loss of our community as we make our scattered way across diverse lands.

> ... The embodied, physical, and cognitive act of writing a cover letter tailored to a specific institution might include researching that institution, department, or city where it is located; considering how this relocation might affect existing relationships; taking in institutional missions and values and considering how these values line up with one's own; getting to know faculty through their departmental profile or professional website and thinking about them as potential colleagues, considering their work in relation to one's own; viewing and co-constructing images that represent possible futures; finding the language to locate oneself within particular programs, departments, universities, or towns; and inscribing these new relational circuits into a two- or three-page single-spaced cover letter.
> —Jennifer Sano-Franchini[1]

The decision to join a community is never solely rational. We discover a way of life we find appealing, learn more about it, start to make friends with others who hold similar values. We shift our vocabulary, our terms of engagement, our enthusiasms. Our calendars are marked by different constraints—rather than birthdays and Thanksgiving, we attune ourselves to semesters, grant proposal deadlines, the week of our discipline's national conference.

We become new people in order to join this new culture. We know that our proposed membership in that community will be subject to great competition. We offer ourselves as contestants in a pageant for people who can't even describe their own desires. We imagine that with the right costume or the right theme music, we might be chosen. We sniff the air, hoping for a phrase to borrow, to learn this year's color, to please the tastemakers as we pass by in the parade of the damned, hoping for the rare and unpredictable nod that will allow us to move from the slush pile to the long list to the short list to the campus visit to—dare we think it?—an offer of membership.

Some few will get in. Some larger number will not. But the peculiar cruelty of higher education is its third option—the vast purgatory of contingent life, in which we are neither welcomed nor rejected, but merely held adjacent to the mansion, to do the work that our betters would prefer not to do.

> The prospect of intellectual freedom, job security, and a life devoted to literature, combined with the urge to recoup a doctoral degree's investment of time, gives young scholars a strong incentive to continue pursuing tenure-track jobs while selling their plasma on Tuesdays and Thursdays.
> —Kevin Birmingham[2]

Again, the rationalists might say that we should walk away, that we should refuse to support an industry that behaves as it does. But intellectual work, paradoxically, is not solely rational. It is a form of desire. It is our identity. It is a community that we love, that does not love us back. So we build a dysfunctional story in which we have at least some role, in which we can name a way that we belong. And the industry is happy to help us manufacture that story, since it keeps us close and useful for a little while longer.

> And so you might conclude that you need to redeem the encounter within a narrative that you may not like but in which you can at least actively participate. This might mean engaging in consensual sex afterward, to make you feel like you wanted it the first time, though you know you didn't. Or staying friendly with the man in the hopes

that you'll find out that he actually did value you, and he wasn't just hoping for access to your body. Or even trying to get something out of the transaction, whatever you can. This looks like weakness, but it's an attempt to gain control.
   —Jia Tolentino[3]

A life of contingency, like any life with an abusive partner, requires us to manufacture elaborate emotional defenses. We imagine that if only we do something better, love will follow. We fear retribution, and so walk quietly. We are uncertain even of our most basic survival if we were to leave, knowing that a few thousand dollars per course is horrible, but having no other readily visible market for our labors. Participation in contingency may look like weakness, but it's an attempt to gain control, to claim a tenuous foothold on the raw, crumbling face of the chasm.

   I used to want to change the world. Now I just want to leave the room with a little dignity.
   —Lotus Weinstock[4]

I have been periodically asked by friends if I'd applied for a college presidency or a provost position they'd seen come open. While I appreciate their graciousness and optimism, I can scarcely think of any jobs I'd want less. My goals were always more modest. I wanted to teach and to write. That was all.

I have two good friends who have both recently become college presidents. One visited our neighborhood last fall, as she and her husband were dropping one of their kids off at a nearby college. And as part of a long and wide-ranging dinner conversation with her and her family, blessedly little of which was about higher ed, she did happen to mention that she'd discovered how much money her school spends on the athletic department. "For that kind of money, we ought to be doing better," she said.

And that little interchange, twenty seconds or so, illuminated perfectly for me exactly why I have never wanted to be a college president. I'm not especially interested in women's soccer or men's golf. I've never wanted to be responsible for real estate, or for negotiations with the host city over contributions to the fire department and EMTs who respond to campus events. I've never wanted to run a private police department, a health center, a sexual assault response team, a legal department, or an advertising department. I've never wanted to oversee a server farm and wireless network, a campus bus system, an off-campus travel policy, or an insurance agency. I went into higher ed because I was selfish, because I wanted to be a teacher and a writer, because those things mattered to me. I can't imagine giving all that up, really for the rest of my life, to wrangle about corporate branding and trustee relations.

But like any addict, I have to be vigilant whenever higher ed calls again. I know what it means to be a member of that cult, to believe in the face of all evidence, to persevere, to serve. I know what it means to take a 50 percent pay cut and move across the country to be allowed back inside the academy as a postdoc after six years in the secular professions. To be *grateful* to give up a career, to give up economic comfort, in order to once again be a member.

Part of me still wants it. That kind of faith is in my bones, and reason can only bleach it away somewhat. The imprint is still there, faint, hauntingly imprecise, all the more venerable for its openness to dreams. I worked as a college administrator for seven years after that postdoc, because I couldn't bear to be away from my beloved community even after it had set me aside. Because I couldn't walk away.

All cults, all abusers, work the same way, taking us away from friends and family, demanding more effort and more sacrifice and more devotion, only to find that we remain the same tantalizing distance from the next promised level. And the sacrifice normalizes itself into more sacrifice, the devotion becomes its own reward, the burn of the hunger as good as the meal.

TRACKING THE ELEMENTS OF CULTURE CHANGE

In this book I've made the argument that a great number of components have changed in ways that collectively make contingency a normal part of the higher education landscape. That's what culture is—innumerable individual choices that mutually make up a way of life.

In this appendix, I'll lay out then-and-now comparisons of what I believe to be some indicators of that culture change. None of them suffice on their own to "explain" contingency, but together with the arguments that I make through the book, I think they give us powerful suggestions of the changing ecosystem that we now inhabit. Think of these data as a basic laboratory panel that might lead you to ask some more specific questions about areas of particular concern.

TABLE 9 Oversupply of new prospective faculty

Argument: Increased numbers of prospective new faculty have increased the competition for tenure-tracked jobs, at the same time as the number of those jobs is in decline.

Then (1976): 32,511	New PhDs[1]	Now (2016): 54,904
Then (1976): 317,477	New master's degrees[2]	Now (2012): 754,229
Then (1999): 240	Number of doctoral degree-granting institutions[3]	Now (2016): 328
Then (2005): 1,193	Tenure-track job postings in the humanities[4]	Now (2016): 552
Then (1976): 68.6%	Percentage of all faculty who are full-time[5]	Now (2016): 49.3%

1. National Center for Science and Engineering Statistics, National Science Foundation, "Survey of Earned Doctorates."
2. National Center for Education Statistics, US Department of Education.
3. National Center for Education Statistics, US Department of Education.
4. Modern Language Association, *Report on the MLA Job Information List, 2015–16*. There should be more efforts like this across a greater array of disciplines.
5. National Center for Education Statistics, US Department of Education.

TABLE 10 Changing income streams for colleges

Argument: The formerly stable mix of tuition, state payments, and gifts and interest has shifted, and colleges have to deal with a less predictable income. In addition, science funding and financial investment are increasing as business components when compared to education, and thus are absorbing more institutional attention and resources.
Note: All calculations are adjusted for inflation.

Then (1988): $3,190	Average public in-state four-year tuition[1]	Now (2018): $9,970
Taking 1986 as a starting point	State funding per FTE[2]	Now (2016): Down 17.2%
Then (1976): $6.7 billion	University income from federally funded research[3]	Now (2015): $23.6 billion
Then (1993): $144 billion	Total market value of college endowments[4]	Now (2014): $535 billion

1. College Board, "Trends in College Pricing."
2. College Board, "Trends in College Pricing."
3. American Association for the Advancement of Science, "Historical Trends in Federal R&D."
4. National Center for Education Statistics, US Department of Education. See also Hsiu-Ling Lee, "The Growth and Stratification of College Endowments in the United States," *International Journal of Educational Advancement* 8, no. 3-4 (September 2008): 136–51.

TABLE 11 Changing demographics of undergraduate education

Argument: As the college population becomes more diverse, and as colleges become more understanding of differences in life experience and needs, more forms of student service are provided by a larger nonfaculty professional staff. (It's also possible that a more diverse student body isn't as readily supported by legislators.)

Then (1976): 47.3% women	More female students[1]	Now (2015): 56.3% women
Then (1976): 15.7% students of color	Fewer white students	Now (2015): 42.4% students of color
Then (1980): 38% of students age 25 and over	More "nontraditional" students	Now (2015): 41% of students age 25 and over
Then (1990): 30%	Higher proportion of high school students with learning disabilities who enroll in college[2]	Now (2005): 48%

1. Data in the first three rows in this table from National Center for Education Statistics, US Department of Education.
2. Cortelia and Horowitz, *The State of Learning Disabilities*, 3rd edition (2014).

TABLE 12 Fluctuating enrollments

Argument: With enrollments cycling up and down, contingent faculty allows for easier "right-sizing" of the teaching force to meet unpredictable student body size. Community colleges especially have been hurt by enrollment collapse, and rely the most on contingent instruction.

Then (1980):	Part-time students	Now (2015):
41% part-time		39% part-time
High (2010):	Peaks and valleys of undergraduate enrollment in the	Low (2015):
18,082,427	past ten years	17,036,778
High (2010):	Peaks and valleys of two-year college enrollment in the	Low (2016):
7,683,597	past ten years	6,090,245

Source: National Center for Education Statistics, US Department of Education

TABLE 13 Mobile students

Argument: As students increasingly choose any school anywhere, and increasingly take transfer credits with them as they move about, introductory courses are more subject to commoditization, are relatively uniform in concept and content, and can be produced at low cost by less well-trained faculty. Schools also have to invest more in recruiting, as they attempt to poach one another's native regional student bodies and defend their own.

Then (1972 cohort):	Transfer students[1]	Now (2008 cohort):
21%		37%
Then (2004):	Out-of-state students	Now (2014):
25%	(sample of 100 public universities)[2]	33%

1. Current data from National Student Clearinghouse; historical data from National Center for Education Statistics, "Transfer Students in Institutions of Higher Education" (1980).
2. Nick Anderson and Kennedy Elliott, "At 'State U.,' a Surge of Students from Out of State." *Washington Post*, January 26, 2016. https://www.washingtonpost.com/graphics/local/declining-in-state-students/.

TABLE 14 Shifts in undergraduate majors

Argument: The shift toward overt career-preparation degrees increases the fluidity of faculty to meet changing technological and economic conditions. The traditional disciplines of liberal education have not increased at the same pace as the overall growth of higher ed; the more technical and career-oriented disciplines have grown more rapidly than average. The faster-growing majors also tend to be more voracious consumers of technology, thus increasing nonfaculty expenses per student.

Then (1976):	Total bachelor's degrees awarded per year	Now (2016):
925,746		1,920,718 (107% increase)
41,452	English and literature	42,795 (3% increase)
126,396	Social sciences and history	161,230 (28% increase)
15,984	Mathematics and statistics	22,777 (42% increase)
19,236	Chemistry, geology, and physics	27,977 (45% increase)
29,630	Engineering	70,104 (137% increase)
53,885	Health professions	288,896 (436% increase)
5,652	Computer science	64,405 (1,040% increase)

Source: National Center for Education Statistics, US Department of Education

TABLE 15   Increase in professional, nonfaculty, nonexecutive staff

Argument: Higher ed is adding new nonfaculty professional positions at a rapid pace; faculty and nonprofessional support staff roles are more often being outsourced. Although the proportion of "full-time faculty" remains stable at 21 percent, that category includes the growing proportion of full-time NTTs, far more common now than before. The great reduction in nonprofessional staff is largely the result of colleges purchasing more of their maintenance, housekeeping, food service, and security services from external vendors.

Then (1991):		Now (2016):
2,545,235	Total higher education employment	3,928,596
535,623 (21%)	Full-time faculty	815,760 (21%)
290,629 (11%)	Part-time faculty	732,972 (19%)
144,755 (6%)	Executive, administrative, and managerial	259,267 (7%)
197,751 (8%)	Graduate student assistants (TAs and RAs)	376,043 (10%)
426,702 (17%)	Nonfaculty professionals	986,621 (25%)
949,775 (37%)	All nonprofessionals	755,917 (19%)

Source: National Center for Education Statistics, US Department of Education

TABLE 16   Increasing managerial compensation

Argument: As colleges and universities become more complex and patterns of income seeking become more diverse, compensation for senior leadership has increased.

Then (2008):		Now (2015):
9	Number of private university presidents at compensation of $1 million or greater	58
Then (2010):	Number of public university presidents at compensation of $1 million or greater	Now (2016):
1		8

Source: Bauman, Davis, and O'Leary, "Executive Compensation at Private and Public Colleges."

TABLE 17 Shifting interest from producer to consumer

Argument: As we become ever more savvy and demanding consumers, we are encouraged to disregard the conditions under which our goods and services are made.

Then (2000):	Number of Americans who shop online[1]	Now (2016):
22%		79%
Then (2006):	Cumulative number of Yelp reviews[2]	Now (2018):
100,000		155,000,000
Then (1983):	Percent of wage and salary workers in unions[3]	Now (2017):
20.1%		10.7%

1. Smith and Anderson, "Online Shopping and E-Commerce."
2. 2006 data from Hillary Dixler Canavan, "Yelp Turns 10," *Eater*, August 5, 2014; 2018 data from Yelp factsheet, March 1, 2018.
3. Bureau of Labor Statistics, US Department of Labor.

TABLE 18 Hope labor

Argument: In a competitive labor market, individuals work for less than market value, often for no compensation at all, in order to "get a foot in the door" as a strategy for hoped-for compensation in a next career stage.

Then (2006):	Uploaded videos per day to YouTube[1]	Now (2013):
20,000		1,000,000
Then (2010):	ISBNs for self-published books per year[2]	Now (2015):
152,978		727,125

1. Golnari, Li, and Zhang, "What Drives the Growth of YouTube?" Proceedings of the sixth ASE International Conference on Social Computing, 2014.
2. Bowker/ProQuest, "Self-Publishing in the United States, 2010–2015."

TABLE 19 The gig economy

Argument: As many as 150 million people work in the gig economy in the United States and Europe. The notion of pickup work rather than full employment is increasingly a normalized part of our economic structure, even as the meager income isn't widely publicized.

Year founded		Average monthly earnings
Uber 2009 Lyft 2012	Gig work as a cab driver	Uber $365 Lyft $377
Airbnb 2008 . . . Getaround 2009	Gig work as a property manager and leasing agent	Airbnb $924 Getaround $98
Doordash 2009 Postmates 2011	Gig work as a delivery carrier	Doordash $229 Postmates $174
TaskRabbit 2008 Etsy 2005	Gig work as a craftsperson/tradesperson	TaskRabbit $380 Etsy $151

Source: Erika Fry and Nicolas Rapp, "This Is the Average Pay at Lyft, Uber, Airbnb, and More," *Fortune*, June 27, 2017. Note that these data are only for vendors who applied for small-business funding; the overall community of gig workers almost certainly makes less.

TABLE 20 Women in the profession

Argument: As a profession becomes more open to women, that profession's salaries decline, working conditions become poorer, and independence is decreased.

Then (1987): 33.2%	Proportion of women in the faculty (not differentiated as full-time versus part-time)[1]	Now (2016): 49.3%
Then (1981): professor, 90%; assoc. prof, 95%; asst. prof, 95%; instructor, 96%; lecturer, 88%; no rank, 90%	Pay gap between male and female faculty at varying ranks (women's pay as a percentage of men's pay)[2]	Now (2016): professor, 85%; assoc. prof, 93%; asst. prof, 92%; instructor, 96%; lecturer, 91%; no rank, 93%
Then (1986): 35.4%	Proportion of women among research doctoral recipients[3]	Now (2016): 46.0%
Then (1981): 50%	Proportion of women among master's degree recipients[4]	Now (2016): 59%

1. National Center for Education Statistics, US Department of Education.
2. National Center for Education Statistics, US Department of Education.
3. Survey of Earned Doctorates, National Science Foundation.
4. National Center for Education Statistics, US Department of Education.

TABLE 21 Educational technology

Argument: Digital technology in all forms has become an integral part of both social and institutional life, and colleges have responded by making these technologies almost globally available. Higher education is particularly impacted by technology spending because of the need for research capability and students' professional training.

Then (2010): $815	Median central IT spending per person (FTE students and employees) across all college types;[1] note that "central IT" does not include department-specific technology in labs or classrooms.	Now (2015): $917
Then (2010): 62.6 million	Increased demand for wi-fi; number of smartphone users in US	Now (2017): 224.3 million
Then (2002): 66	Number of nursing schools using high-fidelity mannequins in simulation laboratories[2]	Now (2010): 917

1. 2015 EDUCAUSE Core Data Service Benchmarking Report.
2. Zak Jason, "A Brief History of Nursing Simulation," Connell School of Nursing, Boston College, May 25, 2015. https://www.bc.edu/bc-web/schools/cson/cson-news/Abriefhistoryofnursingsimulation.html.

TABLE 22 Boomer effects

Argument: The baby boom (1946–64) cohort was so large, in comparison to those before and after it, that it has placed unique demands on public services at every point in its life path—from childhood to college, from parenthood to retirement. The sheer disproportionate size of this demographic bulge has often caused its needs to be prioritized over those of other age cohorts.

Then (1964): 192 million	Total US population	Now (2017): 325 million
Then (1964): 67	Youth dependency rate (people under 18 for every 100 adults age 18–64)	Now (2011): 37
Then (1964): 18	Old-age dependency rate (people 65 and older for every 100 adults age 18–64)	Now (2015): 25

Source: US Census

THE ACADEMIC CAREER
CALIBRATION PROTOCOL

In 1983, Paul Fussell published a funny, marvelous book simply titled *Class*. In it, he included an exercise he called "The Living-Room Scale." The reader started at one hundred points, adding and subtracting points for various items found in their living room to come to an ultimate determination of her or his family's status as working-class proletarian or upper-class bourgeois. The magazines on the coffee table could gain points (*Paris Match, The New York Review of Books*) or lose points (*Popular Mechanics, Field and Stream*). The art on the walls could gain points (original or reproduction work by contemporary artists) or lose points (paintings made by any member of your family).

In a similar vein, I would like to offer a useful scale to help graduate-student readers or their fretful parents understand their pending academic careers. Perhaps more important, if you're at the beginning of your graduate school endeavor, you can use this calibration as a series of markers to work toward. You might only be at 80 points now, but maybe in three years you could be at 250 . . . and now you'll know how the scoring works.

Begin with a score of 100 points, adding and subtracting the specified number of points related to your answers to the following questions. Then look at the scale provided at the end of the protocol to discover your most likely academic career path.

Note: When using the word "discipline," I refer to common, department-scaled content-area divisions. Psychology, for instance, is a discipline; behavioral, environmental, and developmental psychology are subdisciplines. English is a discipline; composition/rhetoric, literature, and creative writing are subdisciplines.

1. I identify as
   - male .... +26
   - female, childless, lesbian .... +4
   - female, childless, straight, single .... +2
   - female, childless, straight, partnered .... −8
   - female, with children .... −10
   - nonbinary/other 0

It seems that the fact of being female doesn't work against higher-ed job seekers so much as the fact of having primary responsibility for childrearing, even if the kids are at that moment still hypothetical. So men get lots of points, because they'll never have to take the lead, and lesbian women get a few points, because the (often mistaken) presumption is that they're safe from kids. Anything else is a risk.

2. My graduate program is
   - in the top twenty schools worldwide for my discipline .. +18
   - outside the top twenty .... −12
   - outside the top fifty .... −26
   - I don't know its ranking .... −36

The only people who ever get good jobs come from the elite schools. And if you don't know your program's ranking, it doesn't speak well for your other preparation.

3. My discipline is offered as an undergraduate major in _____ US colleges.
   - two thousand or more .... +2
   - one to two thousand .... +12

- five hundred to a thousand . . . . −6
- fewer than five hundred . . . . −16
- my program is one of a dozen or less nationwide . . . . −30

The sweet spot is a thousand or two. If your discipline is a major everywhere (English, say, or math), then all the undergrad course credits will be transferrable commodities, and there will be no end of less qualified people who can still teach the intro courses, both of which put downward pressure on the need for hiring.

4. I will be _____ years of age at the completion of my PhD.
- under 30 . . . . +8
- between 30 and 32 . . . . +4
- between 32 and 34 0
- between 34 and 37 . . . . −6
- between 37 and 40 . . . . −10
- older than 40 . . . . −14

If you finished your PhD below the age of thirty, you moved straight from high school to college to grad school, and have all of the life advantages that implies. If you've taken a more circuitous route, you'll scare people off. The committee can't legally ask why, but they'll guess, and the guesses won't be flattering.

5. I have presented my research [add the sum of all that apply]
- at the major national conference in my discipline . . . . . . +10
  - if more than once . . . . +16
- at a smaller national conference . . . . −2
- at a regional disciplinary conference 0
- at an interdisciplinary conference . . . . −8

Not only is it important intellectually to have presented at your major conference, it's also socially beneficial. More people will know who you are. If you're willing to operate outside the mainstream of your discipline, your loyalty is open to question.

6. My dissertation advisor is
   - world-renowned in my discipline .... +24
   - nationally known in my discipline .... +14
   - known within a subfield of my discipline .... −2
   - not well known in my discipline .... −16

The bigger the bodyguard, the more clubs you'll get into.

7. My dissertation advisor
   - is a long-time part of the inner circles of our national
     scholarly organization .... +16
   - is surrounded by friends and colleagues at national
     conferences .... +14
   - has a few close friends at national conferences .... +6
   - is kind of a wallflower at conferences .... −12
   - is actively avoided at conferences .... −22
   - doesn't attend conferences .... −18

The more people who trust and like your sponsor, the more that sponsorship is worth.

8. My dissertation advisor
   - is a vocal fan of me and of my work .... +14
   - doesn't care much one way or the other, or doesn't
     expend much effort .... −8
   - dislikes me or thinks my work is marginal .... −16

The potential energy implied by items 6 and 7 has to be converted into kinetic energy somehow. Will your sponsor provide that spark?

9. My parents are/were involved in the _____ economy.
   - resource (farming, fishing, timbering, mining, etc.) .... −18
   - industrial (manufacturing, shipping, warehousing,
     mechanical) .... −14

- personal service (hairdresser, waitress, receptionist, K-12 ed, etc.) .... −14
- professional (medicine, law, design, publishing, etc.) .... +8
- executive/financial (investment, brokerage, corporate exec, etc.) .... +6
- college faculty or administration .... +24

Fluency in the languages of professional life broadly, and higher ed specifically, is expected. If white-collar life is a second language, you need to practice a lot. Get a copy of my guidebook *The PhDictionary*, for starters.

10. My parents went to [in a two-parent family, your score is the average of the two]
   - the same colleges as their parents .... +18
   - one or both went to the same college as me .... +14
   - a selective college, but one without family history ...... +8
   - a less-than-selective college .... −4
   - community college/trade school .... −12
   - high school .... −24

This is related to item 9, but it measures the specific tribal affiliations of social class as it applies to educational membership. Not educational *attainment*—we expect that—but *membership*. You've got to demonstrate that you're "clubbable," and that's a generational trait.

11. I went to college as an undergraduate
   - in a state other than my home state .... +12
   - in my home state, as a residential student at a private school .... +8
   - in my home state, as a residential student at a public school .... −12
   - in my home state, living at home .... −26

Another social class question, but having to do with whether you and your family were willing to investigate educational options, and whether you had the financial wherewithal to do anything with what you learned.

12. I went to graduate school
  - immediately upon finishing undergrad .... +6
  - after working in a professionally related position for a year or two .... +2
  - after working in an unrelated position for a year or two .... −10
  - after working in any position for more than two years .. −14

This is related to question 4 (age at completion of PhD), but less about privilege than about loyalty. Mucking about in the world of (shudder) commerce marks one as mercenary rather than loyal to the monastic order.

13. As a graduate student [add the sum of all that apply],
  - I have been involved in externally-funded research ...... +8
  - I have been involved in non-funded or internally-funded research 0
  - I have been author or co-author on major-journal peer-reviewed papers .... +8 each
  - I have been author or co-author on small-journal peer-reviewed papers .... +4 each
  - I have written or helped to write successful research funding proposals . . .
    - for $30,000 or less .... +4 each
    - for $30-$100,000 .... +10 each
    - for more than $100,000 .... +22 each
  - I have been approached by academic publishers interested in my dissertation .... +8

This is where the individual merit comes in. Have you, as a graduate student, been a demonstrably productive scholar? You'll need to show a research record to get hired that your senior colleagues would have had to produce for tenure, so start early.

14. Upon completion of my PhD,
- I am geographically unrestricted . . . . o
- I am geographically bound, but within 50 miles of a top-10 metropolitan area . . . . −10
- I am geographically bound, more than 50 miles from a top-10 metro . . . . −44

Does this need explanation? All searches are national searches. If you can't or won't move, you rule out the vast majority of jobs.

15. My parents
- gave me genetically perfect straight teeth . . . . o
- took me to an orthodontist as a child . . . . +4
- wanted to take me to an orthodontist, but couldn't really afford it . . . . −8
- would never have imagined that orthodontics made any difference in life . . . . −16

Like question 11, this is a combination of both resources and family imagination.

16. The average height for American men is roughly 5'10"; for women, 5'4". My height is
- ±2" of the national norm . . . . o
- 2" to 4" above the national norm . . . . +4
- 2" to 4" below the national norm . . . . −8
- more than 4" out of range above . . . . +2
- more than 4" out of range below . . . . −12

A substantial body of research shows that height positively corre-lates with income. You don't want to stand out too far, but you'd do well to rise above the bar.

17. The "ideal" body weight, expressed in BMI, is roughly 20. Mine is
- below 15 . . . . 0 for women, –8 for men
- 15 to 20 . . . . +4 for women, –2 for men
- 20 to 25 . . . . –2 for women, +6 for men
- 25 to 30 . . . . –12 for women, –4 for men
- at or above 30 . . . . –18 for both

This is just broadly cultural. Men should be "solid," and women "slender." Fat shaming is the only prejudice we can still engage in, our culture's guilty pleasure.

18. I have tattoos
- nowhere 0
- nowhere that my coworkers will ever see, thank you very much 0
- occasionally visible at work
  - words/hearts/anchors/skulls etc. . . . . –8
  - tribals/geometrics/ironic intent . . . . +4
- visible in every social situation . . . . –22

The old codgers on the hiring committee would like to think of themselves as a little bit hip, so tattoos that are both subtle and artis-tic might be of use. Tattoos that mark you as working-class, or that can't be hidden, are doom. As the folk wisdom advises, "never get a tattoo where the judge can see it."

19. When I speak,
- no one would be able to guess where I was born and raised 0
- my regional origin is occasionally evident . . . . +6

- my regional origin is strongly evident .... −18
- my British origin is strongly evident .... +12

Whether the accent is Carolina Southern or Southie Irish, Scots Canadian or Bengali, the fact of having an accent will be endearing if it inflects a few vowel sounds now and then, and will mark you as a nonmember if we have to listen to it all the time. Test: Record your voice, play the recording for people you don't know, and ask them where they think the voice comes from. If there's general agreement, you're in trouble. We still think the English sound smarter than we do, though, so there's your one exception.

20. My terminal degree is/will be
- PhD 0
- EdD .... −8
- professional doctorate .... −14
- terminal masters (MFA, MBA, MSW, etc.) .... −22
- academic masters (MA, MS) .... −36

In a crowded market, if you don't start at the top, it's hard to rise there. As a practical note, fewer jobs will be open to applicants without doctorates.

Scoring: With the starting point of your scoring at 100, the highest possible score is over 350, depending on how many publications and grant-funded projects you were able to name in item 13. The lowest possible score is −318. Table 23 shows how your score sets your career trajectory.

At the end of my doctoral education, my score (even including the hundred free points) would have been −14. That explains a lot.

TABLE 23 Predictions of academic career outcomes

	Seeking work at . . .		
Score	Elite research schools	Affluent, creative liberal arts schools	Middle-class and working-class schools
275+	You'll be competitive.	You'll be sought after.	You'll be intimidating.
225–274	You're unlikely to be a serious candidate.	You'll be competitive.	You'll be sought after.
150–224	Forget it.	You're unlikely to be a serious candidate.	You'll be competitive.
75–149	Adjunct possibility, if you have strong professional credentials to go with it.	Forget it.	You're not likely to be at the top of that field, but you never know.
0–75	You have no hope of adjuncting at all.	You're right in the heart of adjunctland.	
0 to −50	You're entirely invisible.	You're probably not a great candidate for being an adjunct.	You might pick up a community college course now and then.
−51 and below	Campus security has your photo in the kiosk, with instructions to bar you from campus events.	We'd love to have your kids consider attending here. It's time to start planning *their* academic career, since yours is over.	

ACKNOWLEDGMENTS

A project like this is the work of many people.

It originated in the mind of my editor at the University of Chicago Press, Elizabeth Branch Dyson, who has shepherded this book and its predecessor, *The PhDictionary*, with care and wisdom and good humor throughout. The first book was a gift from the angels; this one took a lot more labor, and I went back to the well four times, working with Elizabeth to shape the work into superior form. The support has extended through the production team at the Press, editors and designers and marketing professionals pulling together to bring the book to life.

The project relies on the knowledge, both overt and tacit, that I've gained by hanging around with friends in higher ed for twenty years: the tavern stories that let me know how the game was really played. There are far too many people to thank comprehensively, but I'll name a few who have been most central in making me smarter: Bill Campbell, Andrea Chapdelaine, Simon Cook, Iain Crawford, Andy Harris, Nancy Hensel, Van Hillard, Jeanne Mekolichick, Beth Paul, Diana Ramirez-Jasso, Julio Rivera, Kathleen Cown Rood, Jim Ryan, Jenny Shanahan, Ed Toomey. Each of their versions of this story would be different from mine, but I hope they see at least a little of their own thinking embedded within it.

This book has its specificity through interviews and conversations with dozens of people. I won't be naming any of them here, as they're still engaged in the day-to-day social interactions of higher education, and thus can't afford to be seen as contrarians. Some are administrators who can't surrender their one tool for suasion, which is goodwill; many are adjuncts and postdocs who can't offend those who will decide whether to hire them again. I will say that, as part of a community that supposedly values intellectual freedom, I regret that we're so timid about meaningful self-critique, and that we give so few of our colleagues their turn at Speakers' Corner without reprisal.

The project was reborn after my time at the Bread Loaf Writer's Conference, with my thoughtful, generous workshop leader Peter Ho Davies. I was there to work on a novel, but the things I learned about storytelling more broadly have brought this book to a better place.

The project lives because of the support of my wife, my colleague, my first reader, my hero, my fellow castaway, Nora Rubinstein Ph-fucking-D. She enlightened me twenty-five years ago with a brilliant conference presentation, and continues to do that in a thousand new ways. The rule in our house is that only one of us can be crazy at a time; she has more than fulfilled her stable side of the bargain as this book has passed through me. She inspires me daily.

And the project is not finished. You have work to do yourselves, from whatever role you play within the ecosystem. I hope you now know where the predators are, and how to take greater control over the resources you consume and those you provide. The health of the lake is in your hands.

NOTES

NOTES TO CHAPTER ONE

1   Frederickson, "There Is No Excuse for How Universities Treat Adjuncts."
2   *The Economist*, "The Disposable Academic."
3   Jacobs, Perry, and MacGillvary, "The High Public Cost of Low Wages."
4   Kovalik, "Death of an Adjunct."
5   Martichoux, "High Cost of Living Forces San Jose State Professor to Live in Car."
6   Gee, "Facing Poverty."
7   Kelsky, "Sexual Harassment in the Academy."

NOTES TO CHAPTER TWO

1   American Association of University Professors, *Visualizing Change*.
2   Coalition on the Academic Workforce, "A Portrait of Part-Time Faculty Members."
3   Tuttle, "New College Grads."
4   House Committee on Education and the Workforce, *The Just-in-Time Professor*.
5   American Association of University Professors, "Higher Education at a Crossroads."
6   You can use the National Center for Education Statistics "College Navigator" tool at https://nces.ed.gov/collegenavigator/ to find any accredited school in the United States and its territories. The faculty numbers reported here were as of fall 2016.
7   National Center for Education Statistics, "Total Undergraduate Fall Enrollment in Degree-Granting Institutions."
8   National Center for Education Statistics, "Number of Faculty in Degree-Granting Postsecondary Institutions."
9   *Chronicle of Higher Education*, "Contract Lengths of Non-Tenure-Track Faculty

Members." As of fall 2015, 17 percent of all NTTs were on multiyear contracts, 34 percent on single-year contracts, and 49 percent on less than one-year contracts.

10   American Association of University Professors, "Higher Education at a Cross-roads," 14, figure 2.

11   National Center for Education Statistics, "Fall Enrollment Full Instructions," Reporting Directions Part F: Student-to-Faculty Ratio.

12   Schibik and Harrington, "Caveat Emptor." See also the Center for Community College Student Engagement's findings (in *Contingent Commitments*) that part-time faculty are far more likely to teach remedial or "developmental" courses than their full-time peers at community colleges.

13   National Student Clearinghouse Research Center, "Snapshot Report: First-Year Persistence and Retention."

14   Gavillan College, "Career Technical Education."

15   University of California, "Berkeley Research Excellence."

16   Duke University, "Culture of Champions."

NOTES TO CHAPTER THREE

1   Labaree, *A Perfect Mess*, p. 80.

2   Anyon, "Social Class."

3   National Center for Education Statistics, "Total Undergraduate Fall Enrollment in Degree Granting Postsecondary Institutions."

4   Redford and Hoyer, *First-Generation and Continuing Generation College Students*.

5   Ma and Baum, "Trends in Community Colleges."

6   Kruvelis, Cruse, and Gault, "Single Mothers in College."

7   Center for Postsecondary Research, "2015 Update."

8   See Blagg and Chingos, *Choice Deserts*; Hillman and Weichman, *Education Deserts*.

9   College Board, "Average Published Undergraduate Charges."

10   Chen, "Why Community College Students Are Taking Classes at Midnight."

11   We're learning from research what we already knew from everyday experience; namely, that classes meeting once a week for three hours are generally less effective than those meeting for shorter and more frequent sessions. See Cotti, Gordanier and Ozturk, "Class Meeting Frequency, Start Times, and Academic Performance."

12   Rodriguez, Mejia, and Johnson, *Determining College Readiness*.

13   Mangan, "A Simpler Path."

14   National Center for Education Statistics, *Community Colleges*.

15   *Chronicle of Higher Education*, "Adjunct Salaries, 2-Year Public."

16   National Student Clearinghouse, "Snapshot Report: First-Year Persistence and Retention."

17   Jenkins and Fink, "Tracking Transfer."

18   Center for Postsecondary Research, *2015 Update*.

19   Hurlburt and McGarrah, *The Shifting Academic Workforce*.

20   See, for instance, the Higher Learning Commission, "Determining Qualified Faculty."

21   The literature on how small-town education leads toward generalists and big-city education leads toward specialization goes back at least as far as the early 1960s, with Roger Barker and Paul Gump's research in Kansas which led to their book *Big School, Small School* (1964), and their development of the concept of staffing theory.

22   All faculty counts from National Center for Education Statistics, "College Navigator," Fall 2016.

23   For an overview, see Supiano, "Relationships Are Central to the Student Experience."

24   The technical term for these schools is Research 1 Universities, or "Doctoral University, Highest Research Activity" in the Carnegie Classification System. You can look up the classification for a school under "basic classification" at http://carnegieclassifications.iu.edu/. Anybody within higher ed will respond to the term "R1" with the same schools I have just listed.

25   Carnevale, Jayasundera, and Gulish, *America's Divided Recovery*.

26   Burning Glass Technologies, "Moving the Goalposts"; Goodman and Soble, "Global Economy's Stubborn Reality." The phenomenon is also spreading beyond those with college attainment, as graduate degrees are also "worth less" than they once were; see Green and Zhu, "Overqualification."

27   Perhaps literally life-threatening: see Brown and Fischer, "A Dying Town."

NOTES TO CHAPTER FOUR

1   Benton, "Graduate School in the Humanities: Just Don't Go."

2   Bousquet, *How the University Works*.

3   National Science Foundation, *Survey of Earned Doctorates*.

4   This is obviously an approximation. In National Center for Education Statistics, "Number of Faculty in Degree-Granting Postsecondary Institutions," data shows that the number of "full-time" faculty (remember our earlier caveat on that) has increased by about thirty thousand every two years since 2003. Roughly half of those new full-time jobs will be NTT, so the thirty thousand becomes fifteen thousand TT jobs every two years. But that's a gross increase, which means that we have to add some filling of lines for retirements just to stay level. Another way of thinking about it, from a study conducted in engineering, showed that the average professor produces 7.8 new doctorates over the course of her or his career, far too many for simple replacement and system growth (Larson, Ghaffarzadegan and Xue, "Too Many PhD Graduates"). You can start to see why this is complex enough that nobody tracks it—and depressing enough that nobody wants to do so (June, "Why Colleges Still Scarcely Track PhDs").

5   National Research Council, *A Data-Based Assessment of Research-Doctorate Programs in the United States*.

6   For an overview of this literature, see Piper and Wellmon, "How the Academic Elite Reproduces Itself"; Wellmon and Piper, "Publication, Power, and Patronage."

7   This top-ten list is my own summary of their much more subtle methodology; the authors of this study are careful to not make rankings but simply report what

their colleagues thought about one another's programs. I'm under no such need to be considerate.

8   This is only an American list, of course. There are wonderful research colleges around the world, many of whom are contributing their own PhDs to the American job market. A doctoral graduate in mathematics from Oxford, for instance, would be a direct analogue to one from NYU or Berkeley.

9   For studies that demonstrate this reputational power, see Clauset, Arbesman, and Larremore, "Systematic Inequality and Hierarchy in Faculty Hiring Networks"; Amir and Knauff, "Ranking Economics Departments Worldwide on the Basis of PhD Placement"; and Claypool et. al., "Determinants of Salary Dispersion."

10   There's a significant amount of commentary about this from people with experience in faculty hiring. See, for instance, Cawley, "Job-Market Mentor," and Kelsky, "The Professor Is In."

11   Council of Graduate Schools, "University Leaders Issue Statement on Interdisciplinarity in Graduate Education and Research."

12   Raschke, "'There Are No Jobs.'"

13   This is not merely true of the PhD, but of other terminal degrees that are thought to make one eligible for college teaching. See, for instance, Simon, "Why Writers Love to Hate the M.F.A." in which we see that three to four thousand Master of Fine Arts degrees in creative writing are issued every year, with 112 creative writing TT faculty postings for the 2014–15 academic year.

14   Emmons, "Older Workers Account for All Net Job Growth since 2000."

15   Goldsmith, Komlos, and Gold, *The Chicago Guide to Your Academic Career*.

16   The definition of "strong undergraduate program" in this circumstance is surprisingly skewed toward liberal arts colleges like Reed, Swarthmore, Bard, and Grinnell, all of which send a far higher proportion of their graduates to doctoral programs than do the big universities. See Reed College, "Doctoral Degree Productivity." Having one's broad curiosity fostered as an undergrad is recognized as beneficial for focused curiosity later on.

17   Wood, "Who Lands Tenure-Track Jobs?"

18   See also Jaschik, "Bias against Older Candidates."

19   Coleman, *Empowering Yourself*.

20   See, for example, Gasman, "The Five Things No One Will Tell You about Why Colleges Don't Hire More Faculty of Color."

21   Sartre, "A Plea for Intellectuals."

NOTES TO CHAPTER FIVE

1   College Board, "Tuition and Fees and Room and Board over Time."

2   Massauchussetts Institute of Technology, "MIT Facts: Financial Data."

3   Western Michigan University, "General Purpose Financial Report 2016."

4   Desrochers and Hurlburt, *Trends in College Spending*. The longer arc is worse; see Archibald and Feldman, "State Higher Education Spending."

5   Vermont State Colleges, "Presentation to the House Appropriations Committee."

6   Fichtenbaum and Bunsis, "Analyzing University and College Financial Statements."

7   Newfield, *Unmaking the Public University.*
8   Pew Research Center, "Sharp Partisan Divisions."
9   Massachusetts Institute of Technology, "MIT Facts: Financial Data."
10   Bunker Hill Community College, "Financial Statements."
11   Harvard College, "A Brief Profile of the Admitted Class of 2021."
12   Massachusetts Department of Higher Education, "2016 Enrollment Estimates."
13   California Community Colleges Chancellor's Office, "Annual/Term Student Count Report."
14   Jaschik, "The 2017 Survey of Admissions Directors."
15   Shapiro et al., *Transfer & Mobility.*
16   In fact, the fungible transfer credit can be gathered in high school, with an increasing number of students receiving credit for advanced placement courses. See College Board, "Class of 2016 Data."
17   *The Chronicle of Higher Education* has compiled voluntary data from adjuncts across the country at its "Chronicle Data" project (https://data.chronicle.com/). We see three credits of sociology at $2,200 at Northeastern University, $2,300 at Fisher College, $2,760 at Bunker Hill Community College, $3,070 at Mass Bay Community College, and $3,500 at Merrimack College. We've also got Brandeis at $5,000 and Tufts at $6,000; so if you have to adjunct, at least try to do it at a wealthy school.
18   However, that naming is becoming more overt, as student indebtedness threatens to swamp college participants and pressures toward "efficiency" continue to increase. See the "Joint Statement on the Transfer and Award of Credit," co-created by three major higher-ed associations.
19   It's still a flawed market from the students' perspective: the Government Accountability Office ("Students Need More Information") estimates that transferring students lose, on average, about 40 percent of the credits they've accumulated at their originating school. Education consultant Chari Leader ("The Good Business of Transfer") estimates that the cost to students for duplicating nontransferable coursework approaches ten billion dollars a year.
20   National Center for Education Statistics, "College Navigator."
21   Middlebury College, "The Cost of a Middlebury Education."
22   National Center for Education Statistics, "College Navigator."
23   United States Congress, "Act of July 2, 1862 (Morrill Act)"
24   Anft, "The STEM Crisis." See also data from the National Center for Education Statistics showing vast increases in the proportion of undergraduate degrees in engineering, health sciences, and computer science, with languishing degrees in basic science and math.
25   For instance, the Association of Public and Land-Grant Universities, "LIFT, APLU, and NCMS Create Expert Educator Team."
26   National Center for Education Statistics, "Bachelor's Degrees Conferred;" Chace, "The Decline of the English Department."
27   Cited in Smith, "Arkansas College Finds Success in Male-Dominated Fields."
28   Finkelstein, Knight, and Manning, "The Potential and Value of Using Digital Badges for Adult Learners."
29   Desrochers and Kirshstein, *Labor Intensive or Labor Expensive?*, p. 7.
30   US Department of Education, "Strengthening Partnerships."

31   National Center for Education Statistics, "Percentage of Persons 25 to 29 Years Old with Selected Levels of Educational Attainment."
32   Ryan and Bauman, "Educational Attainment."
33   National Association of College and University Business Officers, "U.S. and Canadian Institutions."
34   Cited in Watkins, "Capital Punishment for Midwestern Cities," p. 118.
35   Knight Commission, *Restoring the Balance*.
36   Holbrook and Sanberg, "Understanding the High Cost of Success in University Research."
37   Bauer-Wolf, "Harvey Mudd Cancels Classes."
38   Stewart, "Colleges Need a Language Shift."
39   See the overview from the Indiana University research group: National Survey of Student Engagement, "High-Impact Practices."
40   See, for instance, Field, "Stretched to Capacity."
41   Hensel, ed., "Characteristics of Excellence in Undergraduate Research"; National Postdoctoral Association, "Recommendations for Postdoctoral Policies and Practices"; Campus Compact, "Office for the Community Agenda."
42   Kruvelis, Cruse, and Gault, "Single Mothers in College."
43   Webber and Ehrenberg, "Do Expenditures Other Than Instructional Expenditures. . . ."
44   Boylan, Calderwood, and Bonham, *College Completion*.
45   Desrochers and Hurlburt, *Trends in College Spending*.
46   Center for Community College Student Engagement, *Contingent Commitments*.
47   Delphi Project, "Faculty Matter" and "Review of Selected Policies."
48   Fox, "What Keeps Your Lawyers Awake at Night?"
49   Higher Education Compliance Alliance, "Compliance Matrix."

NOTES TO CHAPTER SIX

1   Frank, *Success and Luck*; Gladwell, *Outliers*.
2   Reed, "Meritocracy and Hiring."
3   American Association of University Professors, "1940 Statement of Principles on Academic Freedom and Tenure." In keeping with the deliberations of academics, they started working on this 850-word statement in 1934.
4   This bifurcation is similar to the longtime adjunct instructor John Warner's differentiation between "tenure as principle," the protector of academic freedom, and "tenure as policy," a mode of labor relations. See Warner, "19 Theses on Tenure."
5   Fischer-Baum, "Is Your State's Highest-Paid Employee a Coach? (Probably)"
6   Flaherty, "Article Sparks New Round of Criticism."
7   State Council of Higher Education for Virginia, "Statement on Civic Engagement."
8   University of North Carolina System, "Economic Engagement."
9   Vermont Agency of Education, "Flexible Pathways."

NOTES TO CHAPTER SEVEN

1   See Council of Graduate Schools/Educational Testing Service, *The Path Forward*, 31, Figure 6.
2   Roach and Sauermann, "The Declining Interest in an Academic Career."
3   Heller, "Contingent Faculty and the Evaluation Process;" Samuels, "Nontenured Faculty Should Not be Assessed by Student Evaluations."
4   Hudd et. al., "Creating a Campus Culture of Integrity"; Isbell, "A Professor Examines Why Her Students Seem to Be So Helpless."
5   Henshaw, "The Challenges for Adjuncts When Supporting and Counseling Sexual Assault Victims."
6   Fry and Rapp, "This is the Average Pay at Uber, Lyft, Airbnb, and More."
7   Dunn, "Colleges Are Slashing Adjuncts' Hours."
8   This has been done, quietly, for a long time. See Ritter, "Ladies Who Don't Know Us Correct Our Papers," for a fascinating overview of the use of "lay readers," women who corrected papers in writing-intensive high school and college courses as far back as the turn of the twentieth century.
9   College for America, "Meet the Advisors & Reviewers."
10   Gary Rhodes was writing about the effects of consumer demand on higher education thirty years ago. See "Higher Education in a Consumer Society." If anything, the effects have accelerated.
11   Industrial Workers of the World, *Unemployment and the Machine*.
12   Toyota Motor Corporation, "How Long Does It Actually Take to Make a Car?"
13   American Honda Motor Company, "Honda Honors its Top North American Suppliers."
14   Kuehn and Corrigan, "Hope Labor."
15   Forbes, "Justin Bieber."
16   Irvine, "Sir Salman Rushdie."
17   "About Grumpy Cat."
18   Brouillette, "Academic Labor."
19   Kreier, "Slaves of the Internet, Unite!"
20   Matthews, "In Gig Economy."
21   Manyika et al., "Independent Work."
22   Cech, "Ideological Wage Inequalities?"
23   Mandel, "Up the Down Staircase." See also Striped Leopard's blog post, "Patriarchy's Magic Trick: How Anything Perceived as Women's Work Immediately Sheds Its Value."
24   Roska, "Double Disadvantage or Blessing in Disguise?"
25   Lincoln, "The Shifting Supply of Men and Women to Occupations."
26   Levanon, England and Allison, "Occupational Feminization and Pay."
27   American Bar Association, *A Current Glance at Women in the Law*; Davidson, "Why Are There More Female Paralegals?"
28   Rhodes and Slaughter, "Academic Capitalism;" Kulis, "Gender Segregation;" Monroe and Chiu, "Gender Equality in the academy."
29   National Center for Education Statistics, "Back to School Statistics."
30   EdTechXGlobal, "Global Report Predicts Edtech Spend to Reach $252bn by 2020."

31   Smith and Lederman, "Enrollment Declines, Transfer Barriers."
32   Marcus, "Many Small Colleges Face Big Enrollment Drops."
33   Earle and Kulow, "The 'Deeply Toxic' Damage Caused by the Abolition of Mandatory Retirement."

NOTES TO CHAPTER EIGHT

1   Federal Water Pollution Control Administration, "The Alewife Explosion."
2   United States Department of Agriculture, "Alewife Species Profile."
3   Eshenroder and Amatangelo, "Reassessment of the Lake Trout Population Collapse in Lake Michigan during the 1940s."
4   Pope, *Colleges that Change Lives*, p.4.
5   I've borrowed this idea from Clare Cooper Marcus and Wendy Sarkissian, in their book *Housing as if People Mattered*.
6   For instance, Commission on Institutions of Higher Education, Standard 4.19, 2016.

NOTES TO AFTERMATH

1   Sano-Franchini, "It's Like Writing Yourself into a Codependent Relationship," 106–7.
2   Birmingham, "The Great Shame of our Profession."
3   Tolentino, Jia, "How Men like Harvey Weinstein Implicate Their Victims in Their Acts."
4   As quoted in the John Cameron Mitchell movie *Shortbus*.

BIBLIOGRAPHY

"About Grumpy Cat." https://www.grumpycats.com/about. Accessed February 22, 2018.

American Association of University Professors. *1940 Statement of Principles on Academic Freedom and Tenure.* Washington: American Association of University Professors. https://www.aaup.org/report/1940-statement-principles-academic-freedom -and-tenure.

———. "Higher Education at a Crossroads: The Economic Value of Tenure and the Security of the Profession: The Annual Report on the Economic Status of the Profession, 2015–16." *Academe,* March-April 2016, 9–23. https://www.aaup.org/sites /default/files/2015-16EconomicStatusReport.pdf.

———. "Visualizing Change: The Annual Report on the Economic Status of the Profession, 2016–17." *Academe* (March-April 2017): 4–26. https://www.aaup.org/file /FCS_2016-17.pdf.

American Bar Association, Commission on Women in the Profession. *A Current Glance at Women in the Law, January 2017.* Chicago: American Bar Association, 2017. https://www.americanbar.org/content/dam/aba/marketing/women/current _glance_statistics_january2017.authcheckdam.pdf.

American Honda Motor Company. "Honda Honors its Top North American Suppliers." *News & Views* (May 3, 2016). http://news.honda.com/newsandviews/article.aspx ?id=8978-en.

Amir, Rabah, and Malgorzata Knauff. "Ranking Economics Departments Worldwide on the Basis of PhD Placement." *Review of Economics and Statistics* 90, no. 1 (2008): 185–90.

Anft, Michael. "The STEM Crisis: Reality or Myth?" *Chronicle of Higher Education* (November 11, 2013). http://www.chronicle.com/article/The-STEM-Crisis-Reality -or/142879.

Anyon, Jean. "Social Class and the Hidden Curriculum." *Journal of Education* 162, no. 1 (winter 1980): 67–92. http://www.jstor.org/stable/42741976.

Archibald, Robert B., and David H. Feldman. "State Higher Education Spending and the Tax Revolt." *Journal of Higher Education* 77, no. 4 (July-August 2006): 618–44. http://www.jstor.org/stable/3838710.

Association of Public and Land-Grant Universities. "LIFT, APLU, and NCMS Create Expert Educator Team to Align Higher Education Curricula with Manufacturing Workforce Needs." *News and Media*, February 22, 2017. http://www.aplu.org/news -and-media/News/lift-aplu-and-ncms-create-expert-educator-team.

Barker, Roger, and Paul Gump. *Big School, Small School: High School Size and Student Behavior*. Palo Alto, CA: Stanford University Press, 1964.

Bauer-Wolf, Jeremy. "Harvey Mudd Cancels Classes after Student Protest over Issues of Race, Workload, and More." *Inside Higher Ed*, April 18, 2017. https://www.inside highered.com/news/2017/04/18/harvey-mudd-cancels-classes-after-student -protests-over-issues-race-workload-and.

Bauman, Dan, Tyler Davis, and Brian O'Leary. "Executive Compensation at Private and Public Colleges." *Chronicle of Higher Education*, July 15, 2018. https://www .chronicle.com/interactives/executive-compensation#id=table_public_2017.

Benton, Thomas H. [William Pannapacker, pseud.]. "Graduate School in the Humanities: Just Don't Go." *Chronicle of Higher Education*, January 30, 2009. https://www .chronicle.com/article/Graduate-School-in-the/44846.

Birmingham, Kevin. "The Great Shame of Our Profession: How the Humanities Survive on Exploitation." *Chronicle of Higher Education*, February 12, 2017. http://www .chronicle.com/article/The-Great-Shame-of-Our/239148.

Blagg, Kristin, and Matthew M. Chingos. *Choice Deserts: How Geography Limits the Potential Impact of Earnings Data on Higher Education*. Washington: Urban Institute, 2016.

Bousquet, Marc. *How the University Works: Higher Education and the Low-Wage Nation*. New York: NYU Press, 2008.

Bowker/ProQuest. "Self-Publishing in the United States, 2010-2015." http://media .bowker.com/documents/bowker-selfpublishing-report2015.pdf.

Boylan, Hunter R., Barbara J. Calderwood, and Barbara S. Bonham. *College Completion: Focus on the Finish Line*. Boone, NC: National Center for Developmental Education, Appalachian State University, 2017. https://ncde.appstate.edu/sites/ncde .appstate.edu/files/College%20Completion%20w%20pg.%201%20per%20bjc%20 suggestion.pdf.

Brouillette, Sarah. "Academic Labor, the Aesthetics of Management, and the Promise of Autonomous Work." Nonsite.org 9 (May 2013). http://nonsite.org/article/aca demic-labor-the-aesthetics-of-management-and-the-promise-of-autonomous-work.

Brown, Sarah, and Karin Fischer. "A Dying Town." *Chronicle of Higher Education*, December 29, 2017. https://www.chronicle.com/interactives/public-health.

Bunker Hill Community College. "Financial Statements and Management's Discussion and Analysis, June 30, 2016." http://www.bhcc.mass.edu/media/01-collegepublica tions/auditreports/BHCC-FY-2016-Final.pdf.

Burning Glass Technologies. "Moving the Goalposts: How Demand for a Bachelor's Degree Is Reshaping the Workforce," September 2014. http://burning-glass.com /wp-content/uploads/Moving_the_Goalposts.pdf.

California Community Colleges Chancellor's Office. "Annual/Term Student Count Report." Management Information Systems Data Mart, accessed February 21, 2018. http://datamart.cccco.edu/Students/Student_Term_Annual_Count.aspx.

Campus Compact. *Office for the Community Agenda: A Model of Campus Support for Community Engagement*. Program Models, accessed February 21, 2018. https:// compact.org/resource-posts/office-for-the-community-agenda-a-model-of -campus-support-for-community-engagement/.

Carnevale, Anthony P., Tamara Jayasundera, and Artem Gulish. *America's Divided Recovery: College Haves and Have-Nots*. Washington: Georgetown University Center on Education and the Workforce, 2016.

Cawley, John. "Job-Market Mentor: The Interdisciplinary PhD." *Chronicle Vitae*, February 23, 2015, https://chroniclevitae.com/news/914-job-market-mentor-the-inter disciplinary-ph-d.

Cech, Erin A. "Ideological Wage Inequalities? The Technical/Social Dualism and the Gender Wage Gap in Engineering." *Social Forces* 91, no. 4 (June 2013): 1147–82.

Center for Community College Student Engagement. *Contingent Commitments: Bringing Part-Time Faculty into Focus*. Austin: University of Texas at Austin, Program in Higher Education Leadership, 2014.

Center for Postsecondary Research. *2015 Update Facts & Figures*. Indiana University School of Education, February 2016. http://carnegieclassifications.iu.edu/down loads/CCIHE2015-FactsFigures-01Feb16.pdf.

Chace, William M. "The Decline of the English Department: How It Happened and What Could Be Done to Reverse It." *American Scholar* 78, no. 4 (Autumn 2009): 32–42. http://www.jstor.org/stable/41222100.

Chen, Grace. "Why Community College Students Are Taking Classes at Midnight." *Community College Review*, September 4, 2017. https://www.communitycollege review.com/blog/why-community-college-students-are-taking-classes-at-midnight.

Chronicle of Higher Education. "Adjunct Salaries, 2-Year Public." *Chronicle Data*. https:// data.chronicle.com/category/sector/4/adjunct-salaries/.

Clauset, Aaron, Samuel Arbesman, and Daniel B. Larremore. "Systematic Inequality and Hierarchy in Faculty Hiring Networks." *Science Advances* 1 (2015). http:// advances.sciencemag.org/content/1/1/e1400005.

Claypool, Vicki Hesli, Brian David Jannsen, Dongkyu Kim, and Sara McLaughlin Mitchell. "Determinants of Salary Dispersion among Political Science Faculty: The Differential Effects of Where You Work (Institutional Characteristics) and What You Do (Negotiate and Publish)." *PS: Political Science and Politics* 50, no. 1 (January 2017): 146–56. https://doi.org/10.1017/S104909651600233X.

Coalition on the Academic Workforce. *A Portrait of Part-Time Faculty Members: A Summary of Findings on Part-Time Faculty Respondents to the Coalition on the Academic Workforce Survey of Contingent Faculty Members and Instructors*. June 2012. http://www.academicworkforce.org/CAW_portrait_2012.pdf.

Coleman, Harvey J. *Empowering Yourself: The Organizational Game Revealed*. Atlanta: Coleman Management Consultants, 1996.

College Board. "Average Published Undergraduate Charges by Sector, 2016–17." https://trends.collegeboard.org/college-pricing/figures-tables/average-published -undergraduate-charges-sector-2016-17.

———. "Class of 2016 Data." https://reports.collegeboard.org/ap-program-results /class-2016-data.

———. "Trends in College Pricing 2017." https://trends.collegeboard.org/sites /default/files/2017-trends-in-college-pricing_1.pdf.

———. "Tuition and Fees and Room and Board over Time, 1976–77 to 2016–17, Selected Years." https://trends.collegeboard.org/college-pricing/figures-tables /tuition-and-fees-and-room-and-board-over-time-1976–77_2016-17-selected-years.

College for America. *Meet the Advisors & Reviewers: Learning and Development Support from Coaches and Academic Reviewers.* Southern New Hampshire University, 2017. http://collegeforamerica.org/for-students/learning-and-development-coaches-and -reviewers/.

Commission on Institutions of Higher Education, New England Association of Schools and Colleges. *Standards for Accreditation*, revised 2016. https://cihe.neasc.org/sites /cihe.neasc.org/files/downloads/Standards/Standards_for_Accreditation.pdf.

Cooper Marcus, Clare, and Wendy Sarkissian. *Housing as if People Mattered.* Berkeley: University of California Press, 1988.

Cortiella, Candace, and Sheldon H. Horowitz. *The State of Learning Disabilities: Facts, Trends and Emerging Issues.* New York: National Center for Learning Disabilities, 2014.

Cotti, Chad, John Gordanier, and Orgul Ozturk. "Class Meeting Frequency, Start Times, and Academic Performance." *Economics of Education Review* 62 (2018): 12–15. http://dx.doi.org/10.1016/j.econedurev.2017.10.010.

Council of Graduate Schools, "University Leaders Issue Statement on Interdisciplinarity in Graduate Education and Research," September 10, 2014. http://cgsnet.org ˙/sites/default/files/press_release_2014_Global_Summit_final.pdf.

Council of Graduate Schools and Educational Testing Service. *The Path Forward: The Future of Graduate Education in the United States.* Report from the Commission on the Future of Graduate Education in the United States. Princeton NJ: Educational Testing Service, 2010.

Delphi Project. *Faculty Matter: Selected Research on Connections between Faculty-Student Interaction and Student Success.* University of Southern California, Delphi Project, 2013. https://pullias.usc.edu/wp-content/uploads/2013/10/Delphi-NTTF _Annotated-Research-Summary_2013WebPDF.pdf.

———. *Review of Selected Policies and Practices and Connections to Student Learning.* University of Southern California, Delphi Project, 2013. https://pullias.usc.edu/wp -content/uploads/2013/07/Delphi-NTTF_Conditions-Student-Summary_2013 WebPDF.pdf.

Desrochers, Donna M., and Steven Hurlburt. *Trends in College Spending: 2003–2013: Where Does the Money Come From? Where Does It Go? What Does It Buy*? Washington: American Institutes for Research, Delta Cost Project, 2016.

Desrochers, Donna M., and Rita Kirshstein. *Labor Intensive or Labor Expensive? Changing Staffing and Compensation Patterns in Higher Education.* Washington: American Institutes for Research, Delta Cost Project, 2014.

Duke University, "Culture of Champions." Duke Undergraduate Admissions, accessed February 20, 2018. http://admissions.duke.edu/experience/champions.

Dunn, Syndi. "Colleges Are Slashing Adjuncts' Hours to Skirt New Rules on Health-Insurance Eligibility." *Chronicle of Higher Education*, April 22, 2013. http://www .chronicle.com/article/Colleges-Curb-Adjuncts-Hours/138653/.

Earle, Beverley, and Marianne DelPo Kulow. "The 'Deeply Toxic' Damage Caused by the Abolition of Mandatory Retirement and its Collision with Tenure in Higher Education: A Proposal for Statutory Repair." *University of Southern California Interdisci-plinary Law Journal* 24, no. 2 (January 2015): 369–418. http://gould.usc.edu/why/students/orgs/ilj/assets/docs/24-2-Earle.pdf.

The Economist. "The Disposable Academic," December 16, 2010. http://www.economist.com/node/17723223.

EdTechXGlobal. "Global Report Predicts Edtech Spend to Reach $252bn by 2020." May 25, 2016. http://www.prnewswire.com/news-releases/global-report-predicts-edtech-spend-to-reach-252bn-by-2020-580765301.html.

Emmons, William. "Older Workers Account for All Net Job Growth since 2000." Federal Reserve Bank of St. Louis, January 15, 2018. https://www.stlouisfed.org/on-the-economy/2018/january/older-workers-account-almost-all-job-growth-2000.

Eshenroder, Randy L, and Kathryn L. Amatangelo. "Reassessment of the Lake Trout Population Collapse in Lake Michigan during the 1940s," Technical Report 65. Ann Arbor: Great Lakes Fishery Commission, 2002.

Federal Water Pollution Control Administration. *The Alewife Explosion: The 1967 Die-Off in Lake Michigan,*. Chicago: Federal Water Pollution Control Administration, 1967.

Fichtenbaum, Rudy, and Howard Bunsis. "Analyzing University and College Financial Statements: How Faculty Can Understand More about University and College Finances." Presentation at the American Association of University Professors Summer Institute, 2014. http://www.hartford.edu/academics/faculty/aaup/files/Appendix-III-Rudy_Howard_Financial_Overview_SI_2014_final.pdf.

Field, Kelly. "Stretched to Capacity: What Campus Counseling Centers Are Doing to Meet Rising Demand." *Chronicle of Higher Education*, November 6, 2016. http://www.chronicle.com/article/Stretched-to-Capacity/238314.

Finkelstein, Jonathan, Erin Knight, and Susan Manning. *The Potential and Value of Using Digital Badges for Adult Learners.* Washington: American Institutes for Research, 2013. https://lincs.ed.gov/publications/pdf/AIR_Digital_Badge_Report_508.pdf.

Fischer-Baum, Reuben. "Is Your State's Highest-Paid Employee a Coach? (Probably.)" *Deadspin Sports*, May 9, 2013. https://deadspin.com/infographic-is-your-states-highest-paid-employee-a-co-489635228.

Flaherty, Colleen. "Article Sparks New Round of Criticism of Costs Associated with Academic Conferences." *Inside Higher Ed*, July 25, 2017. https://www.insidehighered.com/news/2017/07/25/article-sparks-new-round-criticism-costs-associated-academic-conferences.

Forbes. "Justin Bieber." Profile, June 12, 2017. https://www.forbes.com/profile/justin-bieber/.

Fox, Lori E. . "What Keeps Your Lawyers Awake at Night?" *Trusteeship*, September/October 2016. https://www.agb.org/trusteeship/2016/septemberoctober/what-keeps-your-lawyers-awake-at-night#.

Frank, Robert H. *Success and Luck: Good Fortune and the Myth of Meritocracy.* Princeton, NJ: Princeton University Press, 2016.

Frederickson, Caroline. "There Is No Excuse for How Universities Treat Adjuncts." *Atlantic Monthly*, September 15, 2015. https://www.theatlantic.com/business/archive/2015/09/higher-education-college-adjunct-professor-salary/404461/.

Fry, Erika, and Nicolas Rapp. "This Is the Average Pay at Lyft, Uber, Airbnb and More." *Fortune*, June 27, 2017. http://fortune.com/2017/06/27/average-pay-lyft-uber -airbnb/.

Gasman, Marybeth. "The Five Things No One Will Tell You About Why Colleges Don't Hire More Faculty of Color." *Hechinger Report*, September 20, 2016, http:// hechingerreport.org/five-things-no-one-will-tell-colleges-dont-hire-faculty-color/.

Gavilan College. "Career Technical Education." Gavilan College, Academic Programs, accessed February 22, 2018. https://www.gavilan.edu/academic/cte/index.php.

Gee, Alastair. "Facing Poverty, Academics Turn to Sex Work and Sleeping in Cars." *The Guardian*, September 28, 2016. https://www.theguardian.com/us-news/2017/sep /28/adjunct-professors-homeless-sex-work-academia-poverty.

Gladwell, Malcolm. *Outliers: The Story of Success*. New York: Little, Brown, 2008.

Goldsmith, John A., John Komlos, and Penny Schine Gold. *The Chicago Guide to Your Academic Career*. Chicago: University of Chicago Press, 2001.

Golnari, Golshan, Yanhua Li, and Zhi-Li Zhang. "What Drives the Growth of YouTube? Measuring and Analyzing the Evolution Dynamics of YouTube Video Uploads." Sixth annual ASE conference on social computing, 2014. https://www.researchgate .net/publication/263654088_What_Drives_the_Growth_of_YouTube_Measuring _and_Analyzing_the_Evolution_Dynamics_of_YouTube_Video_Uploads.

Government Accountability Office. "Students Need More Information to Help Reduce Challenges in Transferring College Credits." *Report to Congressional Requesters*, GAO-17-574. Washington: Government Accountability Office, 2017. http://www .gao.gov/assets/690/686530.pdf.

Green, Francis, and Yu Zhu. "Overqualification, Job Dissatisfaction, and Increasing Dispersion in the Returns to Graduate Education." *Oxford Economic Papers* 62, no. 4 (2010): 740–63. https://www.kent.ac.uk/economics/documents/GES%20Back ground%20Documents/Overeducation/Overeducation.pdf.

Harvard College. *A Brief Profile of the Admitted Class of 2021*. Harvard College Admissions and Financial Aid, accessed February 21, 2018. https://college.harvard.edu /admissions/admissions-statistics.

Heller, Janet Ruth. "Contingent Faculty and the Evaluation Process." *College Composition and Communication* 64, no. 1 (September 2012): A8–A12. http://www.jstor.org /stable/23264922.

Hensel, Nancy, ed. *Characteristics of Excellence in Undergraduate Research*. Washington: Council on Undergraduate Research, 2012. http://www.cur.org/assets/1/23/COEUR _final.pdf.

Henshaw, Alexis. "The Challenges for Adjuncts When Supporting and Counseling Sexual Assault Victims." *Inside Higher Ed*, June 23, 2017. https://www.inside highered.com/advice/2017/06/23/challenges-adjuncts-when-supporting-and -counseling-sexual-assault-victims-essay.

Higher Education Compliance Alliance. Compliance Matrix. Last updated June 2017. http://www.higheredcompliance.org/matrix/.

Higher Learning Commission. "Determining Qualified Faculty through HLC's Criteria for Accreditation and Assumed Practices.: Last updated March 2016. http://down load.hlcommission.org/FacultyGuidelines_2016_OPB.pdf.

Holbrook, Karen A., and Paul R. Sanberg. "Understanding the High Cost of Success in

University Research." *Technological Innovation* 15 (December 2013): 269–80. doi: 10.3727/194982413X13790020922068.

House Committee on Education and the Workforce, Democratic Staff. *The Just-in-Time Professor: A Staff Report Summarizing eForum Responses on the Working Conditions of Contingent Faculty in Higher Education.* Washington: United States House of Representatives, 2014.

Hudd, Suzanne S., Caroline Apgar, Eric Franklyn Bronson, and Renée Gravois Lee. "Creating a Campus Culture of Integrity: Comparing the Perspectives of Full- and Part-time Faculty." *Journal of Higher Education* 80, no. 2 (March-April 2009): 146–77. http://www.jstor.org/stable/25511l0.0.

Hurlburt, Steven, and Michael McGarrah. *The Shifting Academic Workforce: Where Are the Contingent Faculty?* Washington: American Institutes for Research, 2016. https://www.deltacostproject.org/sites/default/files/products/Shifting-Academic-Workforce-November-2016_0.pdf.

Industrial Workers of the World, General Executive Board. *Unemployment and the Machine.* Chicago: IWW, June 1934.

Irvine, Chris. "Sir Salman Rushdie: 'Fifty Shades of Grey Makes Twilight Look like War and Peace.'" *Telegraph*, October 9, 2012. http://www.telegraph.co.uk/culture/books/booknews/9596577/Sir-Salman-Rushdie-Fifty-Shades-of-Grey-makes-Twilight-look-like-War-and-Peace.html.

Isbell, Lori. "A Professor Examines Why Her Students Seem to Act So Helpless." *Inside Higher Ed*, March 14, 2017. https://www.insidehighered.com/advice/2017/03/14/professor-examines-why-her-students-seem-act-so-helpless-essay.

Jacobs, Ken, Ian Perry, and Jenifer MacGillvary. *The High Public Cost of Low Wages: Poverty-Level Wages Cost U.S. Taxpayers $152.8 Billion Each Year in Public Support for Working Families.* Berkeley: UC Berkeley Center for Labor Research and Education, 2015. http://laborcenter.berkeley.edu/pdf/2015/the-high-public-cost-of-low-wages.pdf.

Jaschik, Scott. "Bias Against Older Candidates." *Inside Higher Ed*, December 17, 2008. https://www.insidehighered.com/news/2008/12/17/age.

———. "The 2017 Survey of Admissions Directors: Pressure All Around." *Inside Higher Ed*, September 13, 2017. https://www.insidehighered.com/news/survey/2017-survey-admissions-directors-pressure-all-around.

Jason, Zak. "A Brief History of Nursing Simulation." Boston College, Connell School of Nursing, May 25, 2015. https://www.bc.edu/bc-web/schools/cson/cson-news/Abriefhistoryofnursingsimulation.html.

Jenkins, Davis, and John Fink. *Tracking Transfer: New Measures of Institutional and State Effectiveness in Helping Community College Students Attain Bachelor's Degrees.* Community College Research Center, Teachers College, Columbia University, 2016. https://ccrc.tc.columbia.edu/publications/tracking-transfer-institutional-state-effectiveness.html.

"Joint Statement on the Transfer and Award of Credit." American Association of Collegiate Registrars and Admissions Officers, Council for Higher Education Accreditation, and American Council on Education. October 2, 2017. http://www.acenet.edu/news-room/Pages/Joint-Statement-on-the-Transfer-and-Award-of-Credit.aspx.

June, Audrey Williams. "Why Colleges Still Scarcely Track Ph.D.s." *Chronicle of Higher*

Education, August 14, 2016. http://www.chronicle.com/article/Why-Colleges-Still
-Scarcely/237412.

Kelsky, Karen. "The Professor Is In: The Curse of the Interdisciplinary Ph.D.," *Chronicle Vitae*, June 16, 2014, https://chroniclevitae.com/news/548-the-professor-is-in-the
-curse-of-the-interdisciplinary-ph-d.

———. "Sexual Harassment in the Academy: A Crowdsource Survey." https://docs
.google.com/spreadsheets/d/1S9KShDLvU7C-KkgEevYTHXr3F6InTenrBsS9yk
-8C5M/edit#gid=1530077352.

Knight Commission on Intercollegiate Athletics. *Restoring the Balance: Dollars, Values, and the Future of College Sports*. Miami: John S. and James L. Knight Foundation, June 2010.

Kovalik, Daniel. "Death of an Adjunct." *Pittsburgh Post-Gazette*, September 18, 2013. http://www.post-gazette.com/opinion/Op-Ed/2013/09/18/Death-of-an-adjunct
/stories/201309180224.

Kreier, Tim. "Slaves of the Internet, Unite!" *New York Times*, Sunday Review, October 26, 2013. http://www.nytimes.com/2013/10/27/opinion/sunday/slaves-of-the
-internet-unite.html.

Kruvelis, Melanie, Lindsey Reichlin Cruse, and Barbara Gault. *Single Mothers in College: Growing Enrollment, Financial Challenges, and the Benefits of Attainment*, Briefing Paper C460. Washington: Institute for Women's Policy Research, 2017. https://
iwpr.org/publications/single-mothers-college-growing-enrollment-financial
-challenges-benefits-attainment/.

Kuehn, Kathleen, and Thomas F. Corrigan. "Hope Labor: The Role of Employment Prospects in Online Social Production." *The Political Economy of Communication* 1, no. 1, (2013): 9–25.

Kulis, Stephen. "Gender Segregation among College and University Employees." *Sociology of Education* 70, no. 2 (April 1997): 151–73. http://www.jstor.org/stable
/2673161.

Labaree, David F. *A Perfect Mess: The Unlikely Ascendancy of American Higher Education*. Chicago: University of Chicago Press, 2017.

Larson, Richard C., Navid Ghaffarzadegan, and Yi Xue. "Too Many PhD Graduates or Too Few Academic Job Openings: The Basic Reproductive Number R_0 in Academia." *Systems Research and Behavioral Science* 31, no. 6 (2014): 745–50. doi:10.1002/sres.2210.

Leader, Chari A. "The Good Business of Transfer." *New England Journal of Higher Education*, February 10, 2010. http://www.nebhe.org/thejournal/the-good-business-of
-transfer/.

Levanon, Asaf, Paula England, and Paul Allison. "Occupational Feminization and Pay: Assessing Causal Dynamics using 1950–2000 US Census Data." *Social Forces* 88, no. 2 (December 2009): 865–91. http://www.jstor.org/stable/40645826.

Lincoln, Anne E. "The Shifting Supply of Men and Women to Occupations: Feminization in Veterinary Education." *Social Forces* 88, no. 5 (July 2010): 1969–98. http://
www.jstor.org/stable/40927535.

Ma, Jennifer, and Sandy Baum. "Trends in Community Colleges: Enrollment, Prices, Student Debt, and Completion." *College Board Research Brief*, April 2016. https://
trends.collegeboard.org/sites/default/files/trends-in-community-colleges-research
-brief.pdf.

Mandel, Hadas. "Up the Down Staircase: Women's Upward Mobility and the Wage Penalty for Occupational Feminization, 1970–2007." *Social Forces* 91, no. 4 (June 2013): 1183–1207.

Mangan, Katherine. "A Simpler Path, Authors Say, Is Key to Community-College Completion." *Chronicle of Higher Education*, April 7, 2015. https://www.chronicle.com/article/A-Simpler-Path-Authors-Say/229133.

Manyika, James, Susan Lund, Jaques Bughin, Kelsey Robinson, Jan Mischke, and Deepa Mahajan. *Independent Work: Choice, Necessity, and the Gig Economy.* San Francisco: McKinsey Global Institute, 2016.

Marcus, Jon. "Many Small Colleges Face Big Enrollment Drops. Here's One Survival Strategy in Ohio." *Washington Post*, June 29, 2017. https://www.washingtonpost.com/news/grade-point/wp/2017/06/29/many-small-colleges-face-big-enrollment-drops-heres-one-survival-strategy-in-ohio.

Martichoux, Alix. "High Cost of Living Forces San Jose State Professor to Live in Car," *San Francisco Chronicle*, August 31, 2017. http://www.sfgate.com/local/article/High-cost-of-living-forces-San-Jose-State-12164855.php.

Massachusetts Department of Higher Education. "2016 Enrollment Estimates." *Massachusetts Department of Higher Education Data Center*, accessed February 21, 2018. http://www.mass.edu/datacenter/2016enrollmentestimates.asp.

Massachusetts Institute of Technology. "MIT Facts: Financial Data, Fiscal Year 2016." http://web.mit.edu/facts/financial.html.

Matthews, Dewayne, "In Gig Economy, It Takes More Than Grit to Get Ahead." *Lumina Foundation News & Views*, September 7, 2017. https://www.luminafoundation.org/news-and-views/the-stairs-start-at-the-second-floor.

Middlebury College. "The Cost of a Middlebury Education." *Middlebury Admissions*, accessed February 19, 2018. http://www.middlebury.edu/admissions/tuition.

Mitchell, John Cameron, director. *Shortbus.* New York: THINKFilm, 2006.

Monroe, Kristen Renwick, and William F. Chiu. "Gender Equality in the Academy: The Pipeline Problem." *PS: Political Science and Politics* 43, no. 2 (April 2010): 303–8. http://www.jstor.org/stable/40646731.

National Association of College and University Business Officers (NACUBO). "U.S. and Canadian Institutions Listed by Fiscal Year (FY) 2016 Endowment Market Value and Change in Endowment Market Value from FY2015 to FY2016." Revised February 2017. http://www.nacubo.org/Documents/EndowmentFiles/2016-Endowment-Market-Values.pdf.

National Center for Education Statistics. "Bachelor's Degrees Conferred by Postsecondary Institutions, by Field of Study: Selected Years 1970–71 through 2014–15." *Digest of Education Statistics*, Table 322.10. https://nces.ed.gov/programs/digest/d16/tables/dt16_322.10.asp.

———. "Back to School Statistics." *Fast Facts*, https://nces.ed.gov/fastfacts/display.asp?id=372.

———. "College Navigator." https://nces.ed.gov/collegenavigator/.

———. *Community Colleges: Special Supplement to The Condition of Education 2008.* NCES 2008-033. Washington: US Department of Education, 2008. https://nces.ed.gov/pubs2008/2008033.pdf.

———. "Fall Enrollment Full Instructions," *IPEDS 2017–18 Data Collection System,*

2017–18 Survey Materials>Instructions, https://surveys.nces.ed.gov/ipeds/VisIn structions.aspx?survey=6&id=30074&show=all#chunk_1313.

———. "Number of Faculty in Degree-Granting Postsecondary Institutions, by Employment Status, Sex, Control, and Level of Institution: Selected Years, fall 1970 through fall 2013." *Digest of Education Statistics*, table 315.10. https://nces.ed.gov /programs/digest/d15/tables/dt15_315.10.asp.

———. "Percentage of Persons 25 to 29 Years Old with Selected Levels of Educational Attainment, by Race/Ethnicity and Sex: Selected Years, 1920 through 2016." *Digest of Education Statistics*, Table 104.20. https://nces.ed.gov/programs/digest/d16 /tables/dt16_104.20.asp.

———. "Percentage of Recent High School Completers Enrolled in 2-Year and 4-Year Colleges, by Income Level: 1975 through 2015," *Digest of Education Statistics*, table 302.30. https://nces.ed.gov/programs/digest/d16/tables/dt16_302.30.asp.

———. "Race/Ethnicity of College Faculty." *Fast Facts*. https://nces.ed.gov/fastfacts /display.asp?id=61.

———. "Total Fall Enrollment in Degree-Granting Postsecondary Institutions, by Attendance Status, Sex, and Age: Selected Years, 1970 through 2025," *Digest of Education Statistics*, table 303.40. https://nces.ed.gov/programs/digest/d15/tables/dt15 _303.40.asp.

———. "Total Fall Enrollment in Degree-Granting Postsecondary Institutions, by Level of Enrollment, Sex, Attendance Status, and Race/Ethnicity of Student: Selected Years, 1976 through 2015," *Digest of Education Statistics*, table 306.10. https://nces.ed.gov/programs/digest/d16/tables/dt16_306.10.asp.

———. "Total Undergraduate Fall Enrollment in Degree-Granting Postsecondary Institutions, by Attendance sSatus, Sex of Student, and Control and Level of Institution: Selected Years, 1970 through 2026," *Digest of Education Statistics*, table 303.70. https://nces.ed.gov/programs/digest/d16/tables/dt16_303.70.asp.

National Center for Health Statistics. "Vital Statistics of the United States." Centers for Disease Control and Prevention, May 2017. https://www.cdc.gov/nchs/data_access /vitalstatsonline.htm.

National Postdoctoral Association. "Recommendations for Postdoctoral Policies and Practices." Version 7-1-14. Rockville, MD: National Postdoctoral Association, 2014. http://www.nationalpostdoc.org/?recommpostdocpolicy.

National Research Council. *A Data-Based Assessment of Research-Doctorate Programs in the United States.* Washington: National Academies Press, 2011. https://doi.org /10.17226/12994.

National Science Foundation. "Doctorate Recipients from US Colleges and Universities: 1957–2015." *Survey of Earned Doctorates*, table 1. https://www.nsf.gov/statis tics/2017/nsf17306/data/tab1.pdf.

National Student Clearinghouse Research Center. "Snapshot Report: First-Year Persistence and Retention." National Student Clearinghouse, June 12, 2017. https:// nscresearchcenter.org/snapshotreport28-first-year-persistence-and-retention/.

National Survey of Student Engagement (NSSE). "High-Impact Practices." Indiana University Center for Postsecondary Research. http://nsse.indiana.edu/html/high _impact_practices.cfm.

Newfield, Christopher. *Unmaking the Public University: The Forty-Year Assault on the Middle Class.* Cambridge MA: Harvard University Press, 2008.

Pew Research Center. "Sharp Partisan Divisions in Views of National Institutions." *US Politics and Policy*, July 10, 2017. http://www.people-press.org/2017/07/10/sharp -partisan-divisions-in-views-of-national-institutions/.

Piper, Andrew, and Chad Wellmon. "How the Academic Elite Reproduces Itself." *Chronicle of Higher Education*, October 8, 2017. http://www.chronicle.com/article /How-the-Academic-Elite/241374.

Pope, Loren. *Colleges That Change Lives*. New York: Penguin, 1996.

Raschke, Carl. "'There Are No Jobs': Common Fallacies and Facts about Getting an Academic Job in Religion or Theology." *The Other Journal*, November 30, 2014. https://theotherjournal.com/2014/11/30/there-are-no-jobs-common-fallacies-and -facts-about-getting-a-phd-in-religion-or-theology/.

Redford, Jeremy, and Kathleen Mulvaney Hoyer. *First-Generation and Continuing-Generation College Students: A Comparison of High School and Postsecondary Experiences*. NCES 2018–009. National Center for Education Statistics, September 2017. https://nces.ed.gov/pubsearch/pubsinfo.asp?pubid=2018009.

Reed College. "Doctoral Degree Productivity." Reed College Institutional Research, *Facts about Reed*, accessed February 20, 2018. https://www.reed.edu/ir/phd.html.

Reed, Matt [writing under the pseudonym "Dean Dad"]. "Meritocracy and Hiring," *Inside Higher Ed*, "Confessions of a Community College Dean" blog, January 31, 2011. https://www.insidehighered.com/blogs/confessions_of_a_community_col lege_dean/meritocracy_and_hiring.

Rhodes, Gary. "Higher Education in a Consumer Society." *Journal of Higher Education* 58, no. 1 (January-February 1987): 1–24. http://www.jstor.org/stable/1981387.

Rhodes, Gary, and Sheila Slaughter. "Academic Capitalism, Managed Professionals, and Supply-Side Higher Education." *Social Text* 51 (summer 1997): 9–38. http:// www.jstor.org/stable/466645.

Ritter, Kelly. "'Ladies Who Don't Know Us Correct our Papers': Postwar Lay Reader Programs and Twenty-First Century Contingent Labor in First-Year Writing." *College Composition and Communication* 63, no. 3 (February 2012): 387–419. http://www .jstor.org/stable/23131595.

Roach, Michael, and Henry Sauermann. "The Declining Interest in an Academic Career." *PLoS ONE* 12, no. 9 (2017). https://doi.org/10.1371/journal.pone.0184130.

Rodriguez, Olga, Marisol Cuellar Mejia, and Hans Johnson. *Determining College Readiness in California's Community Colleges: A Survey of Assessment and Placement Policies*. San Francisco and Sacramento: Public Policy Institute of California, November 2016. http://www.ppic.org/publication/determining-college-readiness-in-califor nias-community-colleges-a-survey-of-assessment-and-placement-policies/.

Roska, Josipa. "Double Disadvantage or Blessing in Disguise? Understanding the Relationship between College Major and Employment Sector." *Sociology of Education* 78, no. 3 (July 2005): 207–32. http://www.jstor.org/stable/4148915.

Ryan, Camille L, and Kurt Bauman, "Educational Attainment in the United States: 2015." Publication P20–578. Washington: United States Census, March 2016. https:// www.census.gov/content/dam/Census/library/publications/2016/demo/p20-578 .pdf.

Samuels, Robert. "Nontenured Faculty Should Not Be Assessed by Student Evaluations in This Politically Charged Era." *Inside Higher Ed*, April 24, 2017. https://www

.insidehighered.com/views/2017/04/24/nontenured-faculty-should-not-be
-assessed-student-evaluations-politically-charged.

Sano-Franchini, Jennifer. "'It's Like Writing Yourself into a Codependent Relationship with Someone Who Doesn't Even Want You!': Emotional Labor, Intimacy, and the Academic Job Market in Rhetoric and Composition." *College Composition and Communication* 68, no. 1 (September 2016): 98–124.

Sartre, Jean-Paul. "A Plea for Intellectuals." In *Between Existentialism and Marxism,* 228–85. New York: William Morrow, 1976.

Schibik, Timothy, and Charles Harrington. "Caveat Emptor: Is There a Relationship between Part-Time Faculty Utilization and Student Learning Outcomes and Retention?" *AIR Professional File,* #91 (Spring 2004). Washington: Association for Institutional Research. https://files.eric.ed.gov/fulltext/ED512352.pdf.

Shapiro, Doug, Afet Dundar, Phoebe Khasiala Wakhungu, Xin Yuan, and Autumn T. Harrell. *Transfer & Mobility: A National View of Student Movement in Postsecondary Institutions, Fall 2008 Cohort.* Signature Report no. 9. Herndon, VA: National Student Clearinghouse Research Center, 2015.

Simon, Cecelia Capuzzi. "Why Writers Love to Hate the M.F.A." *New York Times,* April 9, 2015. https://www.nytimes.com/2015/04/12/education/edlife/12edl-12mfa .html?_r=0.

Smith, Aaron, and Monica Anderson. "Online shopping and e-commerce." Pew Research Center, December 19, 2016. http://www.pewinternet.org/2016/12/19 /online-shopping-and-e-commerce/.

Smith, Ashley A. "Arkansas College Finds Success in Male-Dominated Fields but Wants Short-Term Pell." *Inside Higher Ed,* August 10, 2017. https://www.inside highered.com/news/2017/08/10/arkansas-college-finds-success-male-dominated -fields-wants-short-term-pell.

Smith, Ashley A., and Doug Lederman. "Enrollment Declines, Transfer Barriers: Community College Presidents' Survey." *Inside Higher Ed,* April 21, 2017. https:// www.insidehighered.com/news/survey/community-college-presidents-surveyed -enrollment-recruitment-pipeline.

State Council of Higher Education for Virginia. "Statement on Civic Engagement." May 31, 2017. http://www.schev.edu/docs/default-source/institution-section /GuidancePolicy/assessment/civic-engagement-meeting-2017/civic-engagement -statement.pdf.

Stewart, Davina-Lazarus. "Colleges Need a Language Shift, but Not the One You Think." *Inside Higher Ed,* March 30, 2017. https://www.insidehighered.com/views /2017/03/30/colleges-need-language-shift-not-one-you-think-essay.

Striped Leopard (pseudonym). "Patriarchy's Magic Trick: How Anything Perceived As Women's Work Immediately Sheds Its Value." December 13, 2013. https:// cratesandribbons.com/2013/12/13/patriarchys-magic-trick-how-anything -perceived-as-womens-work-immediately-sheds-its-value/.

Supiano, Beckie. "Relationships Are Central to the Student Experience. Can Colleges Engineer Them?" *Chronicle of Higher Education,* January 14, 2018. https://www .chronicle.com/article/Relationships-Are-Central-to/242230.

Tolentino, Jia. "How Men Like Harvey Weinstein Implicate Their Victims in Their Acts." *The New Yorker,* October 11, 2017. https://www.newyorker.com/culture/jia -tolentino/how-men-like-harvey-weinstein-implicate-their-victims-in-their-acts.

Toyota Motor Corporation. "How Long Does It Actually Take to Make a Car?" *Children's Question Room,* accessed February 21, 2018. http://www.toyota.co.jp/en/kids/faq/b/01/06/.

Tuttle, Brad. "New College Grads Could Be Looking at the Highest Starting Salaries Ever." *Money,* May 12, 2017. http://time.com/money/4777074/college-grad-pay-2017-average-salary/.

United States Congress. "Act of July 2, 1862 (Morrill Act), Public Law 37–108, Which Established Land Grant Colleges, 07/02/1862." *Enrolled Acts and Resolutions of Congress, 1789–1996*; Record Group 11; General Records of the United States Government; National Archives. https://www.ourdocuments.gov/doc.php?flash=false&doc=33&page=transcript.

United States Department of Agriculture "Aquatic Species: Alewife." National Invasive Species Information Center, last modified July 19, 2017. https://www.invasivespeciesinfo.gov/aquatics/alewife.shtml.

United States Department of Education, "Strengthening Partnerships between Businesses and Community Colleges to Grow the Middle Class," Archived press release, February 5, 2016. https://www.ed.gov/news/press-releases/strengthening-partnerships-between-businesses-and-community-colleges-grow-middle-class.

University of California. "Berkeley Research Excellence; 2016–17 Research Funding Sponsors." https://vcresearch.berkeley.edu/excellence/berkeley-research-excellence.

University of North Carolina System. "Economic Engagement." https://www.northcarolina.edu/serving-locally-and-globally/economic-engagement-0.

Vermont Agency of Education. "Flexible Pathways." http://education.vermont.gov/student-learning/flexible-pathways.

Vermont State Colleges. "Presentation to the House Appropriations Committee, February 2014." http://www.leg.state.vt.us/jfo/appropriations/fy_2015/Department%20Budgets/VSC%20-%20FY%202015%20Budget%20Presentation.pdf.

Warner, John. "19 Theses on Tenure." *Inside Higher Ed,* "Just Visiting" blog, February 21, 2017. https://www.insidehighered.com/blogs/just-visiting/19-theses-tenure.

Watkins, Alfred J. "Capital Punishment for Midwestern Cities." in *The Metropolitan Midwest: Problems and Prospects for Change,* edited by Barry Checkoway and Carl V. Patton, 107–23. Champaign: University of Illinois Press, 1985.

Webber, Douglas A., and Ronald G. Ehrenberg. "Do Expenditures Other Than Instructional Expenditures Affect Graduation and Persistence Rates in American Higher Education?" *NBER Working Paper 15216.* Cambridge: National Bureau of Economic Research, 2009. http://www.nber.org/papers/w15216.pdf.

Wellmon, Chad, and Andrew Piper. "Publication, Power, and Patronage: On Inequality and Academic Publishing." *Critical Inquiry,* updated October 2, 2017. https://criticalinquiry.uchicago.edu/publication_power_and_patronage_on_inequality_and_academic_publishing/.

Western Michigan University. *General Purpose Financial Report, June 30, 2016.* https://wmich.edu/sites/default/files/attachments/u327/2016/wmu_finreport_2016.pdf.

Wood, L. Maren. "Who Lands Tenure-Track Jobs?" https://lilligroup.com/research/.

INDEX